the ^bachelor's tiny kitchen™

the tiny kitchen™ series

bachelor's

the ^tiny kitchen™

a man's guide to cooking and entertaining

with bill

by denise sullivan ^medved

cover illustration by todd healy

TINY KITCHEN PUBLISHING   2004

FIRST EDITION

Designed by Denise Sullivan Medved

Photography copyright © 2003

Rita Maas/Envision: Eggs Benedict; Shrimp Kebab; Roasted Chicken; Broiled Salmon

Steven Mark Needham/Envision: French Onion Soup; BBQ Ribs

Madeline Polss/Envision: Reuben; Cocktail

Cover Illustration by Todd Healy

Library of Congress Control Number 2003090578

ISBN 0-9716028-1-6

Dedicated to my brother ROBERT, affectionately known as Robbie Boy, who definitely could have used this book.

And to my nephews and godsons, Matthew Moran, Patrick Sullivan, Matthew Hennessy, Blake Sanford, Colin Amos Connor Sullivan, Graham Sullivan, Jack Sullivan, Riley Sullivan, Sean Sullivan, Edward Ward, Stephen Ward, all bachelors in the making.

Also dedicated to my nieces, Katie Moran, Madelyn Amos, Amelia Sullivan, Annie Sullivan, Hilary Sullivan, Sarah Sullivan, Susie Sullivan. May this serve as a training manual for your boyfriends.

contents

acknowledgments

the bachelor's tiny kitchen is the second in the *tiny kitchen* series. When I first came up with the tiny kitchen concept, the idea was to create a series of books focused on cooking and entertaining within the confines of a tiny kitchen. I pitched the concept to no less than twenty agents and publishers, none of whom chose to publish it. I decided to pursue the concept myself and self-published *the tiny kitchen cooking and entertaining*. As one might imagine it is a substantial financial commitment and somewhat of a risk, but in my heart I knew there was a market for it. I had no idea how in the world I was going to get rid of the 4,000 copies that were delivered to my garage on December 11, 2001. Needless to say, if the 4,000 copies of *the tiny kitchen* didn't sell, that would be the end of the series. I am proud to say *the tiny kitchen cooking and entertaining* has sold 7,500 copies and is now in its third printing.

Countless people contributed to the success of *the tiny kitchen cooking and entertaining* after it was published. Without its success there would be no *bachelor's tiny kitchen*. I am very grateful and would be remiss if I didn't take the time to acknowledge those responsible:

My husband, Bill, who exhibited tremendous patience with the cartons of books in our garage taking up precious space for all his tools and other guy's stuff.

My mother and father Bob and Kay Sullivan, sister Missy, brother-in-law Bob, niece Katie and nephew Matthew for buying so many copies and promoting the book.

Todd Healy, my friend and the artist whose eye-catching cover illustrations for *the tiny kitchen* motivated people to pick up the book and thumb through it. Also, for selling so many copies at his shop, Gallery Lafayette. Don't you just love this new cover he did? Check out his meatloaf recipe on page 93.

My cousin, Jeri Pinson Wellens, food photographer. What's a cookbook without tempting photographs? If Todd's cover enticed people to pick up the book and thumb through it, the photographs got the book to the cash register.

Kathy Ann White one of my best friends from junior high school. She hosted the first book signing on December 11, 2001 the day 4,000 books were delivered to my garage. That really got the ball rolling!

Stacy Jones another lifelong friend who graciously hosted a book signing the following week, adding to the momentum.

Aunt Loretta who tirelessly and selflessly promoted *the tiny kitchen* wherever possible and single-handedly sold nearly two hundred copies.

Inez Yuri and Kellie Meehan who invited me to their club meetings as guest speaker.

Courtney Monkhouse, Customer Relations Manager at Barnes and Noble in Alexandria, Virginia for inviting me in for a book signing, *and* who featured *the tiny kitchen* in the window display for two weeks!

Bas Bleu Catalog, booksellers-by-post who prominently featured *the tiny kitchen* in their 2002 holiday catalog.

IPG Books, my distributor, chancing it with a first-time self-published author.

Gail Curcio, who wrote the first article about *the tiny kitchen* giving it a full spread, complete with color photos in the *Alexandria Gazette.*

Elizabeth Gaynor, editor of Best Buys column in *Parade Magazine,* who featured *the tiny kitchen* in October 2002, my first national press.

Every one of my friends, family and those whom I don't know, who bought *the tiny kitchen* and recommended it to their friends. Thank you all! Each of these efforts helped sell the book and propelled it into its third printing. I hope you enjoy this book as well.

I express my heartfelt thanks and gratitude to all who contributed to *the bachelor's tiny kitchen*:

My husband Bill for his consultation, recipes, continued love, encouragement and gentle, yet welcome prodding.

My mother and father, who continue to encourage me every step of the way, no matter what the project.

My sister, brother-in-law, nephew and all other relatives who showed a genuine interest and contributed recipes. Especially my niece, Katie, who consulted on the cover colors and design.

Todd Healy, my friend and the artist who created yet another eye-catching cover illustration. Thank you, Todd, for your continued encouragement.

The bachelors (or former bachelors) who contributed recipes to this book: the Boys from Belfast, Hendi and Pauly, George Braun, Todd Healy, Carter Jones, Bill Medved, Mike Pomponio, Tom Rasmussen, Jimmy Schonberger, Bob Sullivan, Dolan Sullivan, John Sullivan, Keith Sullivan, Steve Vito, Lowell Weicker, Jr.

And last, but not least, St. Anthony, St. Rita and St. Jude. I've got the same deal with you for this book.

introduction

Welcome to *the bachelor's tiny kitchen*! The chances are you, the bachelor, did not buy this book yourself. Your mother, sister, girlfriend, friend, child or other relative probably gave it to you as a gift. Am I right?

The bachelor's tiny kitchen isn't really for you—it's really for the person who gave it to you. It's to make them feel good that you, the bachelor, no matter what stage you are in your life, have a resource for cooking and entertaining.

As the gift-giver thumbed through this book in the store, they saw the mouth watering pictures, the variety of recipes, the easy directions and helpful hints, and they had you in mind.

The mother thought, "Oh good. Now my son can eat more than macaroni and cheese and TV dinners. He can eat just like Mama's home cookin'! He might even invite his father and me over for brunch some day."

The girlfriend thought, "Now he has no excuse not to cook a romantic dinner for me or take me on a picnic. It tells him how to do it all right here."

The sister thought, "This will teach him there's more to a guy's kitchen than old pizza boxes and beer. It will actually make him want to spruce things up and learn to cook and entertain. Maybe my brother will finally have a party and serve more than just chips, dip and cans of beer. He might even make a good impression on the girls. One might even stick around for a while."

The child thought, "Even though Dad's alone now and he's not used to fixing his own meals, I'm happy knowing *the bachelor's tiny kitchen* will show him the way and he can still eat well. Plus, there's lots of recipes here I like that we can cook together!"

The friend thought, "He's already such a fabulous cook but there are some great new ideas in here. Plus, it will make a great addition to his cookbook collection or get him started on one."

The bachelor's tiny kitchen was actually written with people who care about you in mind. But it was also written with you, the bachelor, in mind. If your kitchen is only big enough for one cookbook, this should get you through almost any cooking or entertaining situation. It's easy to read, has a variety of ideas and recipes that range from basic, such as scrambled eggs and bacon, to more time consuming such as rustic short ribs.

Although written from a woman's perspective I collaborated with several men, including my husband Bill, to ensure a meaningful and useful variety of recipes and ideas. As you read the stories and anecdotes you will hear Bill chiming in from time to time.

Face it, most women don't give guys credit for being able to do laundry, iron, clean the bathroom, let alone cook! Bill impressed me early on with his domesticity, the clean house, the matching towels in the bathroom and breaded pork chops (page 101). Women love a guy who can cook, or at least will give it a try.

So here you are with your copy of *the bachelor's tiny kitchen.* "What should I do with it?" you might be asking yourself. Well, I have one recommendation: use it. Whether you are a twenty-something just out of college and living on your own, the thirty-something, sophisticated bachelor, the forty or fifty-something who suddenly found yourself a bachelor again this book is for you. There is something in here for everyone. Remember, don't take cooking and entertaining too seriously—it's supposed to be fun! Just enjoy.

bachelor's
the ^tiny kitchen™

a man's guide to cooking and entertaining

the bachelor's kitchen

the term "bachelor's kitchen" typically conjures up images of a fridge with a six-pack (and maybe some sour milk), a cupboard housing a couple of cans of tuna, a few jars of prepared tomato sauce and a box of pasta; a pot; a few mismatched plates, forks and knives and a large spoon for stirring.

Hey, you guys are getting a bad rap. Those whose imaginations immediately flip to this image aren't giving bachelors enough credit. There is an unfounded assumption that most men can't cook. What a fallacy that is. Witness some of the great chefs who are household names: Jacques Pepin, Emeril Lagasse, Jamie Olive, the Naked Chef, Wolfgang Puck and Daniel Boulud. They may not all be bachelors now, but they once were. Granted, not all bachelors are a Jacques or an Emeril, but I happen to believe a fair number of them fall somewhere on the culinary adeptness continuum where my father (who is still not sure which one is the stove and which one is the oven) is one extreme and Jacques is the other. As I was researching this book, I can't tell you how many bachelors (or former bachelors) said to me, "Oh, I've got a great recipe for you."

Bill has been cooking since he was a kid. In fact his chili became famous among Boy Scout Troop 1894. During camp outs the scouts would anxiously await a fresh batch of Billy's Chili prepared over an open campfire.

My first book, *the tiny kitchen cooking and entertaining,* was inspired by my years as a twenty-something, single professional living in Manhattan. I was strapped for cash, time, and space, but loved to cook and entertain. I had a tiny kitchen and needed to make it work. Bill describes *his* first kitchen as follows:

"The vintage kitchen in the apartment I rented during college was basic and functional. It was small, (not quite as tiny as Denise's in her Captain's Row apartment) had the avocado green appliances and could barely fit two people. I picked up some pots and pans at a yard sale and had enough to get by and to prepare nice meals. Of course, there was *always* a pot of chili and a variety of hot sauces in the refrigerator. My landlady did not cook, so I prepared dinner for her a couple of nights a week in exchange for reduced rent."

stocking the bachelor's tiny kitchen

No matter how small your kitchen, you should be able to find room for basic supplies. If necessary, store your pots on the stove top (they stack nicely inside each other) and your pans, pie plates, cookie sheet and baking dishes in the oven like I did. I still store my roasting pans and broiler pan in the oven for old times' sake. When using the oven or stove top, put the pots and pans you're not using on top of the refrigerator, a counter top, or stash them under a table somewhere until you're finished using their "home." Other supplies should fit into one cupboard and one drawer. If you're just getting started in your own kitchen here is a list that will help you stock your kitchen with the basics (get the good stuff; someday it might be incorporated into a tiny kitchen for two!).

cookware

6-inch paring knife	steamer (*metal*)
10-inch knife	tongs
potato peeler	meat thermometer
rubber spatula (*heat resistent*)	set of measuring spoons
pancake turner	2-cup glass measuring cup
hand mixer	4-sided grater
whisk	nest of 4 glass mixing bowls
sieve (*doubles as a sifter and colander*)	cookie sheet
	roasting pan
pastry brush	broiler pan

Dutch oven with lid	2-quart saucepan with lid
8 x 8-inch square baking pan	4-quart saucepan with lid
9-inch pie plate	6-inch skillet
9 x 13-inch glass baking dish	10-inch skillet
6-quart stock pot with lid	

If you at least have these things on hand you'll be cookin'. If you don't, you might want to invest in what you don't have. If you have more than this—great; you have more than I did starting out.

prepared foods

Some foods are just easier to buy prepared than make from scratch, and they are just as good as homemade. Some I always keep on hand and recommend in my recipes include: Newman's Own Olive Oil and Vinegar Dressing, Newman's Own Balsamic Vinaigrette, Swanson Chicken Broth, Swanson Beef Broth, McCormick Sauce Blends (hollandaise, béarnaise, green peppercorn and hunter's), Old El Paso Taco Seasoning and Buitoni Pesto Sauce. (You probably have your own favorites, but these happen to be the ones I use regularly and always have in my cupboard).

I call for many of these in recipes. If a recipe calls for chicken broth or beef broth, I suggest using Swanson. The quality and flavor are very good. Growing up, the only salad dressing I liked was my mother's oil and vinegar. We didn't use any bottled dressings until Newman's Own Olive Oil and Vinegar Dressing came along. I use it religiously now for marinating chicken, beef, fish or lamb or as a salad dressing on green salads, pasta salad and wild rice salad and for coating potatoes I plan to roast. From time to time I will make my own dressing, but ninety-nine percent of the time, it's Newman's Own. For Bill, it's Ken's Steak House Lite Caesar. He loves it so much I tease him that I'm going to make him a Kenny's Cocktail!

By having some staples on hand you can usually whip something up in a pinch, whether it's a snack for unexpected company or a quick dinner.

canned and dry goods	in the fridge	in the freezer
tomato sauce	butter	green beans
tomato paste	milk	corn
Swanson chicken broth	orange juice	ice cream, any
Swanson beef broth	eggs	flavor
tortilla chips	mayonnaise	
pretzels	mustard	
mixed nuts	olives	on the spice rack
pasta	dill pickles	salt
rice	onions	pepper
flour	salsa	parsley flakes
sugar	horseradish	chives
olive oil	Tabasco	onion salt
Newman's Own Olive Oil	Worcestershire sauce	garlic
and Vinegar Dressing	Ken's Steak House Lite	
crackers	Caesar	
McCormick Sauce Blends	pesto	
(hollandaise, béarnaise,	tortellini	
green peppercorn and	celery	
hunter's)	carrots	
taco seasoning mix	a six pack, *of course*	

the bachelor and the hot sauces (a food group of their own)

Hot sauces are in a category of their own. Most men I know have some sort of an affinity for hot sauces. Bill suffers from a chronic, extreme case of *can'tgetitspicyenoughitis* (did you figure that out?). I have never in my life witnessed anyone who can tolerate the level of spiciness he does. Granted, I am highly sensitive to anything spicy; black pepper is my limit and Tabasco sends me into orbit. Bill, on the other hand can tolerate just about anything hot and spicy.

You know how a lot of macho guys will say to the waiter, "Make it as hot as you can—nothin's too hot for me. Bring it on!" So, the chef douses the dish with the hot sauce du jour to the point where it's beyond edible, just to teach the guy a lesson. The guy takes one bite, his entire body is on fire, and he learned his lesson (until the next time he's feeling macho). Bill isn't one of those guys. Honest, he really can take the heat, so to speak. But he has tremendous respect for the one sauce he can only take in small doses— Dave's Insanity Sauce. We bought a bottle right after we were married from a cart vendor at Baltimore's Inner Harbor. The guy selling it warned Bill to use it sparingly; very sparingly. He suggested only the tip of a toothpickful for one bowl of chili. Bill heeded his advice and as a result has never been "burned" by Dave's Insanity Sauce. It took him nearly eight years, but Bill finally finished that bottle—this from a man who consumes a restaurant size bottle of Tabasco a month. That's how hot it is. I dare you to try it.

We went skiing a few years ago at Big Mountain, Montana. There is a great bar at the base of the mountain called The Stube where everyone gathers for aprés ski to enjoy drinks, snacks, kitchy entertainment, and to recount the last run of the day. The Afterburner Burger is a popular menu item; it's a hamburger served with Dave's Insanity Sauce, a fire extinguisher and a fire helmet, really. All those who order the Afterburner Burger must sign a disclaimer something to the effect of, "Management is not responsible for anyone eating the Afterburner Burger." Those who eat an entire Afterburner Burger are honored with their picture posted on the wall behind the bar showcasing the elite few who accomplished the same feat, and a tee shirt that reads, "I survived The Afterburner Burger at the Stube." Though many have tried, few have succeeded.

We were in The Stube one afternoon and Bill, knowing the intensity of Dave's

Insanity Sauce, ordered it confessing to the waiter this was the only hot sauce he truly considered dangerous. The amount of sauce slathered on is directly proportional to the machoism of the patron.

When the Afterburner Burger is delivered to the table it is done so with a fair amount of pomp and circumstance—all eyes in the restaurant are on the diner—the waiter crowns him with the fire helmet, places the burger and extinguisher in front of him and wishes him luck. A "macho" guy witnessing Bill's ceremony, was curious about all the fuss, and boasted eating the Afterburner Burger would be a piece of cake for him. He ordered the burger and was treated to the same ceremony Bill received.

It took about an hour, but Bill managed to finish the Afterburner Burger and his coronation was an equally impressive ceremony. All eyes once again on him as he slipped into his new red tee shirt and had his picture taken, then posted on the wall of honor.

Several hours after we left The Stube we stopped in for a night cap. The "macho" guy was still sitting there, in agony, staring at a half-eaten Afterburner Burger, determined to get the tee shirt and his picture on the wall. When we left, he was still sitting there.

To this day Bill says the Afterburner Burger is the hottest thing he has ever eaten in his entire life. And, he has the tee shirt to prove it.

Just for giggles I ran into the kitchen to see what Bill has in terms of hot sauces in the fridge that are open, and on active rotation for him to use in doctoring up what he considers my "bland" cooking. Here's what I found taking up residence: Chili Garlic Sauce, Cholula Hot Sauce, Crystal Wing Sauce, Green Tabasco, Maui Pepper Company Mango Meltdown, Melinda's Original Habanaro Pepper Sauce, XXXXtra Reserve, Ocracoke Pirate Sauce, Sriracha Hot Chili Sauce, Sweat Thang, Tabasco, Chipolte, Tabasco Habanaro Sauce, Try Me Cajun Sunshine Hot Pepper

Sauce, Try Me Tiger Sauce, Wild Cat Sauce, Wine and Pepper Sauce, Wy's Wings, Dave's Insanity Sauce.

Unless you're a fanatic like Bill, you probably aren't going to have eighteen hot sauces in your refrigerator at once. But he does suggests a few on hand at all times.

eating and serving utensils

I remember my brother Robert telling me stories of his friend Leo. They were classmates at Georgia Tech, engineering majors. Robert used to laugh at how Leo only ate off paper plates and used plastic forks and knives. Leo insisted it was more efficient and made cleanup easy. I guess he had a point—that's an engineer for you!

I would suggest you make a minimal investment in some plates and flatware. There's no need to go overboard in getting things that are too fancy—in fact, don't. The odds are against you that your girlfriend(s) will like what you buy. Remember, she's always evaluating everything about you and the wrong dishes can get a check mark in the wrong column. You can't go wrong with classic white or clear glass dishes. They're very inexpensive and never go out of style. Any food looks good on them. Depending on how much entertaining you plan on doing, invest in six, eight or twelve place settings.

pieces in a place setting	suggested serving pieces
dinner plates	serving bowl (*oven proof*)
salad plates	2 small bowls for nuts, chips, etc.
bread and butter plates	serving tray
forks	serving fork
knives	2 serving spoons
spoons	salt and pepper shakers

classics from the ^original tiny kitchen ™

billy's chili - 14

guacamole - 16

roasted garlic - 17

bill's cole slaw - 18

brooklyn potato salad - 19

mashed potatoes - 20

baked potatoes - 20

sea salt roasted potatoes - 21

grains - 22

roasted chicken - three ways - 24

pasta bolognese - 27

beef burgundy - 28

whole roasted beef tenderloin - 29

broiled filet mignon with sautéed mushrooms - 30

broiled balsamic lamb chops - 31

the tiny kitchen cooking and entertaining, (the first book in the tiny kitchen series) included many of my favorite recipes. Roasted chicken, mashed potatoes, pasta bolognese, beef burgundy, chili—yum! They're classics. I received many compliments from readers on these so I thought I would pass them along in this book.

Bill makes a batch of chili and I roast a chicken once a week just to have in the refrigerator so there's always something on hand for a quick meal. On occasion we forget about it and it gets pitched once it resembles a science experiment.

These recipes will get you by in almost any situation and people will love these all-time favorites. I hope you enjoy these personal favorites.

billy's chili
serves 6

Before I met Bill I had never tasted chili. I don't care for beans and I thought all chili was chock full of beans. Bill's chili does not call for beans but you can certainly add them. The first couple of times he made chili for me it was too spicy. If you follow this recipe as written you'll find it may have a little kick; if it's too much just leave out the cayenne pepper. This is a true winner—all of our friends rave about it. For our annual Black and Blue Bowl Party (a flag football game the Saturday before Thanksgiving) Bill makes the equivalent of ten batches. We serve it after the game along with a hot sauce bar (Bill has about eighteen different hot sauces) and it's usually gone within the hour.

3 tablespoons vegetable oil
3 onions, chopped
3½ pounds of ground beef
6 tablespoons chili powder
2 cans (28 ounces each) tomato sauce
1 can (6 ounces) tomato paste
1 can (12 ounces) beer
¼ teaspoon basil
2 bay leaves
2 teaspoons fresh ground black pepper
cayenne pepper to taste
1½ tablespoons cilantro
2 tablespoons cumin powder

¾ teaspoon garlic powder
1½ teaspoons Italian seasoning
1 teaspoon paprika
1 tablespoon parsley
crushed red pepper taste
1 tablespoon sugar
¼ teaspoon tarragon
3 tablespoons Worcestershire sauce
½ cup cider vinegar
Tabasco
shredded cheddar cheese
chopped onions
diced jalapeno peppers

Heat oil in a stockpot over medium high heat. Sauté onions until tender; approximately 3 – 4 minutes. Add ground beef and brown. While the meat is browning add the chili powder. Once the meat has browned add the tomato sauce, tomato paste and beer and mix together thoroughly. Stir in the rest of the ingredients, except the cheese, onions and jalapeno peppers (they're for the garnish).

Bring to a boil, cover, then reduce heat, cover and simmer for 3 hours. If the chili becomes too thick, add water or beer to thin it out. Serve in individual bowls and top with cheddar cheese, chopped onions, jalapeno peppers and sour cream. To spice it up a bit add Tabasco and your favorite hot sauces. Bill especially likes Dave's Insanity Sauce. The flavor is enhanced if it's refrigerated overnight, then reheated.

alternative serving suggestions

Serve over cooked pasta shells. The chili seeps into the shells. It's really good. Our friend Carter likes to add some cooked corn to his.

chili dog

Place a boiled or grilled hot dog in a hot dog bun. Smother with chili, onions and cheese.

a note from bill

For years people have raved about my chili. I have never given this recipe out to anyone. The fact that I turned Niecie into a chili lover is testimony to this recipe. It alone is worth the cost of *the tiny kitchen*!

guacamole
serves 10 to 12

Avocados brown quickly once peeled and exposed to the air. Sprinkling them with lemon juice helps to maintain a fresh look and minimize discoloration. To keep guacamole fresh, make within an hour or of your intended serving time.

> 4 very ripe avocados
> juice of 1 lemon or lime
> 10 dashes Tabasco
> ½ teaspoon salt
> ⅛ teaspoon cayenne pepper
> 2 roma tomatoes, seeded and diced
> ½ large red onion, diced
> tortilla chips

Peel and pit the avocados and mash them in a mixing bowl with the lemon or lime juice. Leave some chunks—you don't want it like baby food Add salt, cayenne pepper and Tabasco and mix. Stir in the tomatoes and onions. If you do not plan to serve it immediately, cover with plastic wrap by placing the plastic wrap directly on the surface of the guacamole to keep the air from turning it brown. The flavor is enhanced if it is refrigerated for an hour. Serve with tortilla chips.

roasted garlic
serves 4

The first time I had roasted garlic was on our honeymoon and it seemed to be a popular item on the menu. Bill ordered it as an appetizer (against my wishes) and when it was brought to the table it smelled so good it was irresistible. I think I ate more than he did. We ordered it a few more times that week. When we returned home I decided to put the garlic baker someone had given us for a gift to use. I urge you to try this!

1 head garlic
¼ teaspoon olive oil
¼ teaspoon thyme
salt and pepper to taste
wedge of saga cheese
1 baguette, sliced
4 sprigs of fresh parsley

> When roasted, the garlic has a very creamy texture and a sweet, nutty flavor. It's very easy to remove and spread with a knife or cocktail fork. The combination of the garlic and the goat cheese makes for a very unique taste. The parsley is to be eaten afterward as it eliminates the garlic odor.

Preheat the oven to 350°.

Cut the tops (about ¼-inch) off the garlic to expose the cloves. Drizzle the garlic with olive oil and season with thyme, salt and pepper. Wrap the garlic loosely in aluminum foil, but be sure to close all the sides tightly (of course if you have a garlic baker, use that). Place directly on oven rack and bake for 45 minutes. Arrange the garlic, cheese and baguette slices on a tray. Serve warm by spreading garlic, then goat cheese on baguette slices. Eat the parsley afterwards to freshen your breath.

bill's cole slaw
serves 6

My all time favorite cole slaw was served at Roy Rogers, which also happened to be my favorite fast-food restaurant. McDonald's bought out Roy Rogers several years ago and slowly converted the restaurants to McDonald's. The last Roy Rogers in my area was just closed a few weeks ago. No one's cole slaw could compare to it. It was creamy, but not too mayonnaisey, not too wet, not too sweet and with the perfect balance of spices. Besides the mayonnaise the only ingredient I could identify was celery seed. I tried several times to duplicate their recipe with no success. The first time Bill made cole slaw I couldn't believe it. His tasted just like Roy Rogers! Here it is…

> 4 cups shredded cabbage
> 2 large carrots, shredded
> 1½ cups mayonnaise
> 3 tablespoons cider vinegar
> 2 tablespoons celery seed
> 2 tablespoons sugar
> salt and pepper to taste

In a large bowl combine cabbage and carrots. In a small bowl mix the mayonnaise, cider vinegar, celery seed, sugar, salt and pepper. Combine with cabbage and carrots and mix thoroughly. Chill before serving.

brooklyn potato salad
serves 8 - 10

There are many varieties of potato salad. It seems everyone has their own secret ingredient and I'm not sure there are two alike. My mother learned to make potato salad from my Grandma Dexter and it's the only potato salad she really likes. When my mother tasted for the first time potato salad Bill had made she couldn't believe it—it was just like hers! When she told him, he told her he learned to make it from his mother. His mom was from Brooklyn as was Grandma Dexter. This must be the way they make potato salad in Brooklyn!

5 pounds white potatoes	2 cups mayonnaise
1 cup diced celery	2 tablespoons celery seed
½ cup diced onions	2 tablespoons sugar
2 large carrots, shredded	¼ cup vinegar
3 tablespoons chopped fresh parsley	salt and pepper to taste

Peel, wash and quarter the potatoes and boil for 15 minutes or until fork tender. Drain and let cool for 30 minutes.

Slice the potatoes in ⅛-inch slices into a large bowl. Add the celery, onions and carrots and mix gently. Mix the mayonnaise, celery seed, sugar, vinegar, salt and pepper in a small bowl. Add the mayonnaise mixture to the potato mixture. Mix thoroughly. For maximum flavor refrigerate for an hour before serving. Garnish with parsley. It's even better the next day!

potatoes

old-fashioned mashed potatoes
serves 6

3 pounds white potatoes   1 cup heavy cream
4 tablespoons butter   salt and pepper to taste

Peel, wash and cut the potatoes in quarters. Boil the potatoes in salted water for approximately 15 minutes until fork tender. While potatoes are cooking melt the butter with the heavy cream over low heat. Drain the potatoes. Using a potato masher, mash the potatoes with the butter, heavy cream and salt and pepper until smooth.

baked potatoes
serves 2

2 baking potatoes   sour cream
butter   chives

Preheat the oven to 400°.

Wash the potatoes. Prick the potatoes with a fork in several places (this will keep them from exploding in the oven). Place the potatoes directly on the oven rack. Bake for 1 hour.

To serve, cut lengthwise and load up with butter, sour cream and chives.

sea salt roasted potatoes
serves 6

These potatoes are great. The two tablespoons of sea salt sounds like a lot, but it gives them a delicious flavor. They're crispy on the outside and very soft on the inside. Serve them with roasted chicken, beef tenderloin or pork tenderloin.

3 pounds new red potatoes
½ cup of Newman's Own Olive
    Oil and Vinegar Dressing
2 tablespoons sea salt
fresh ground black pepper to
    taste

Preheat the oven to 400°.

    Wash and cut the potatoes (leaving the skin on) in half or quarters depending on the size to make bite sized pieces. Boil the potatoes in salted water for approximately 8 minutes. Drain the potatoes and let cool for a few minutes. Pour ¼ cup dressing in the bottom of a roasting pan, and coat the pan. Sprinkle 1 tablespoon of sea salt and pepper to taste on top. Place the potatoes, skin side up, and brush the remaining ¼ cup dressing on top of the potatoes to coat. Sprinkle remaining 1 tablespoon of sea salt and pepper to taste over the potatoes. Bake for 30 minutes.

alternative

Put the dressing, salt and pepper in a large plastic bag. Put the raw cut potatoes in the bag. Tie the bag to close and shake vigorously to coat. Put the coated potatoes into the roasting pan and bake at 400° for about an hour.

dilled new potatoes

After boiling the potatoes drain them. Return to the pot and toss with 2 tablespoons butter and 2 tablespoons dill.

grains

Here are basic cooking techniques for several types of rice. Wild rice (which is actually the seed of an aquatic grass) pops open when it's cooked and has a rich brown color and nutty taste and texture. Similarly, brown rice has a nutty taste with a chewy texture. Basmati rice is highly aromatic with a light, sweet taste.

wild rice
serves 6

> 1 box (4 ounces) wild rice
> 2¾ cups chicken broth
> ½ cup diced celery

Rinse rice in cold water in a sieve to remove impurities. Combine rice, chicken broth and celery in a saucepan. Bring to a boil. Reduce heat and simmer covered for 1 hour. Let rice cool.

brown rice
serves 4

> 1 cup brown rice
> 2 cups beef broth
> 1 teaspoon butter

couscous
serves 4

1 cup of couscous
1 cup of chicken broth

Bring chicken broth to a boil in a small saucepan. Stir in the couscous. Cover and remove from heat. Let stand for 5 minutes. Fluff with a fork. Makes 4 cups.

Combine rice, beef broth and butter in a saucepan. Bring to a boil. Reduce heat and simmer covered for 45 minutes. Let rice cool.

basmati rice

serves 4

1 cup basmati rice
2¼ cups water

Bring the water to a boil in a saucepan. Stir in the rice. Reduce heat and simmer covered for 20 minutes until all the liquid has been absorbed.

long grain white rice

serves 4

1 cup long grain white rice
2¼ cups water
½ teaspoon salt
1 teaspoon butter

spanish rice

serves 4

1 cup long grain rice
2 tablespoons vegetable oil
¼ cup chopped onion
1 jalapeno pepper, seeded and diced
4 ounces tomato sauce
2 cups water
½ teaspoon garlic powder
½ teaspoon salt
½ teaspoon pepper

Heat the oil in a saucepan over medium heat. Add the rice and cook until brown, about 5 minutes. Add the onion and jalapeno and sauté for 2 minutes. Add the tomato sauce, water and spices. Bring to a boil. Cover and simmer for 15 minutes until all the liquid is absorbed.

Bring the water to a boil in a saucepan. Add salt and butter. Stir in the rice. Reduce heat and simmer covered for 20 minutes until all the liquid has been absorbed.

For added flavor for rice or couscous add 2 tablespoons of parsley, chives, dill or any other herbs of choice. Mix the herbs with the dry rice or couscous before adding the liquid.

roasted chicken - three ways
serves 4

old fashioned with brown gravy

      1 roasting chicken (4 – 6 pounds)
      2 large carrots cut into large pieces or several baby carrots
      1 onion, quartered
      2 stalks celery cut into large pieces
      salt and pepper to taste
      2 cups canned chicken broth
      chicken stock from giblets
      ½ cup flour

Preheat the oven to 350°.

Remove the giblets and rinse the cavity of the chicken. Put the giblets in a 4-quart pot filled with water. Add half of the carrots, onion and celery. Bring to a boil, then simmer covered for about an hour. This makes a nice homemade stock.

Meanwhile season the chicken with salt and pepper and place in a roasting pan. Add the remaining carrots, onions and celery. Pour 1 cup of chicken broth into the roasting pan. Roast for 20 – 25 minutes per pound, basting every 15 minutes (adding more chicken broth if pan becomes dry). To test whether it's done, pierce the thigh with the tip of a knife. If clear juices run out, it's done. Some birds have a built in timer to indicate when it's done; they are very accurate.

When the giblets have finished cooking, discard them (or cut up and put in the gravy, if you like) and the vegetables. You have a nice rich stock to use in making the gravy. When the chicken has finished roasting, place on a cutting board and let cool while making the gravy.

Place the roasting pan on the stove top but do not turn on the heat. Remove all but three tablespoons of fat from the pan. Add ¼ cup of chicken stock and deglaze the pan scraping up the brown pieces. Stir in the flour until it's well blended (it should have a smooth, paste-like consistency and no lumps). Add 1 cup of chicken stock and blend in, over medium heat, stirring constantly until the gravy thickens. If it becomes too thick add more stock until it's the consistency you like. Adjust the seasoning with salt. Slice the chicken and serve with old-fashioned mashed potatoes (page 20).

roasted chicken with red wine reduction

> 1 roasting chicken (4 – 6 pounds)
> 3 tablespoons chopped fresh rosemary
> salt and pepper to taste
> 2 cups chicken broth
> 1½ cups dry red wine

Preheat the oven to 350°.

Remove the giblets and discard. Season the chicken with salt, pepper and rosemary and place in a roasting pan. Pour 1 cup of chicken broth and ½ cup red wine in the roasting pan. Roast for 20 – 25 minutes per pound, basting every 15 minutes (adding more chicken broth if necessary). To test whether it's done, pierce the thigh with the tip of a knife. If clear juices run out, it's done. Some birds have a built in timer to indicate when it's done; it is very accurate.

When the chicken has finished roasting, place on a cutting board and let cool while making the gravy. Skim the fat from the pan just leaving the juices. Add 1 cup of red wine and deglaze the pan scraping up the brown pieces. Boil down the liquid until it thickens slightly. Adjust the seasoning with salt. Slice the chicken and serve with wild rice and spoon the sauce over top.

chicken with white wine reduction

Prepare chicken as above but eliminate the rosemary and substitute dry white wine for the red wine to make the sauce. Rub the chicken with a garlic clove, then the juice of one lemon. Season with salt and pepper. Roast according to the above instructions. This has a much lighter flavor than with the red wine or the brown gravy.

---

roasted chicken and pesto sandwiches

Leftover roasted chicken sliced makes a great sandwich. I often make these sandwiches for a picnic dinner for outdoor concerts in the park at Wolf Trap.

1 fresh baguette
sliced white meat chicken
2 roma tomatoes, sliced
pesto (*I prefer Buitoni brand found in the refrigerator section*)
fresh mozzarella, sliced

Slice the baguette lengthwise. Spread pesto dipping sauce on the inside top and bottom of the sliced baguette. Place a layer of chicken on the bottom half of the baguette; top with a layer of tomatoes then a layer of mozzarella. Put the top on the baguette. Slice baguette into 2 inch slices.

---

pasta bolognese
serves 6

2 pounds ground beef
2 pounds ground veal
2 tablespoons olive oil
1 onion, diced
2 cloves garlic, minced
1 stalk celery, finely diced
2 cans (29 ounces each) tomato sauce
2 tablespoons basil
2 tablespoons oregano

2 teaspoons salt
1 teaspoon pepper
1 bay leaf
1 cup dry red wine
2 cans (6 ounces each) tomato
   paste
⅛ teaspoon cinnamon
4 cups cooked spaghetti
Parmesan cheese

In a large stockpot brown the beef and veal over medium heat. Remove the meat and set aside. Drain the liquid from the pot. In the same pot heat the olive oil over medium heat. Add the onion, garlic and celery and cook for 5 minutes. Stir in the meat, tomato sauce, basil, oregano, salt, pepper and bay leaf. Simmer covered for 45 minutes.

   In a small bowl mix the tomato paste, red wine and cinnamon until thoroughly blended, and then stir into the meat sauce. Simmer covered for 15 minutes. Remove the bay leaf. Serve over the cooked spaghetti and sprinkle with Parmesan cheese.

beef burgundy

serves 6

4 tablespoons olive oil
½ cup flour
2 teaspoons salt
1 teaspoon pepper
1 teaspoon celery seed
1 teaspoon dried thyme
½ teaspoon marjoram
2 ½ pounds lean beef stew meat
   cut into 1-inch cubes

3 cups beef broth
1 cup dry red wine
1 bay leaf
1 tablespoon Dijon mustard
12 baby carrots
12 small white boiling onions,
   trimmed and peeled
2 large potatoes, peeled and cut into
   1-inch cubes

Heat the olive oil over medium heat in a large stockpot. Mix the flour, salt, pepper, celery seed, thyme and marjoram together in a bowl. Roll the beef cubes in the flour mixture to fully coat the cubes. If there is leftover flour mixture, set aside. Brown the meat a few pieces at a time and set aside.

After browning all the meat add the beef broth, wine, bay leaf and mustard. Return the meat to the pot and cover and simmer for 1½ hours. Add the carrots, onions and potatoes. Cook for 15 – 20 more minutes until the potatoes, carrots and onions are fork tender. Remove the meat, potatoes and vegetables from the pot and cover to keep warm. If there is remaining flour mixture, place it in a small bowl and add 2 tablespoons of water (adding the flour mixture dry directly into the large pot of hot liquid will create lumps in the liquid) and mix until smooth. Then stir this mixture into the pot of liquid. Bring the liquid to a boil to thicken to the consistency you like. Serve in soup bowls with warm crusty bread.

whole roasted beef tenderloin
serves 6 - 8

You can't go wrong with serving beef tenderloin. It's such a flavorful, tender cut of meat that requires little preparation or cooking time. Even though it's a bit more expensive than other cuts of beef, it's well worth it. I offer three of my favorite ways to serve it.

> 1 whole beef tenderloin (6 – 7 pounds)
> Newman's Own Olive Oil and Vinegar Dressing
> salt and pepper, to taste
> McCormick Béarnaise Sauce Mix

Preheat the oven to 425°.

Trim the tenderloin of excess fat and scrappy ends and remove the thin silvery membrane. Brush the tenderloin with the dressing, season with salt and freshly ground black pepper. Put the tenderloin in a roasting pan and roast 30 minutes for rare and 40 minutes for medium-rare.

Prepare béarnaise sauce mix according to the directions on the package. Serve tenderloin sliced with the sauce and assorted steamed vegetables.

---

sliced tenderloin

After roasting the tenderloin let it cool completely. Slice thinly for a cocktail buffet.

---

broiled filet mignon with sautéed mushrooms

serves 2

This is a great alternative to a whole beef tenderloin if you're just having dinner for two.

> 2 filet mignons (1½-inches thick)
> salt and pepper to taste
> 2 tablespoons butter
> ¾ cup sliced white mushrooms
> ¼ cup dry red wine
> 1 package McCormick Green Peppercorn Sauce

Preheat the broiler.

Season the meat with salt and pepper. Place on a broiler pan and broil for 5 minutes per side for rare and 7 – 9 minutes per side for medium.

While the meat is cooking melt the butter in a sauté pan over medium heat. Add the mushrooms and sauté for 2 – 3 minutes. Add the red wine and simmer while the meat is broiling. Prepare the green peppercorn sauce mix according to the instructions on the package. Serve the filet topped with the sautéed mushrooms and sauce.

broiled balsamic lamb chops

serves 2

Lamb is traditionally served with mint jelly or a mint sauce. Try it with the rich hunter sauce; it gives it a very different flavor.

4 lamb chops about 1½-inches thick
Newman's Own Balsamic Vinaigrette
1 package McCormick Hunter Sauce Mix

Preheat the broiler.

Brush the lamb chops with the vinaigrette. Place in a broiler pan and place under the broiler. Broil for 5 minutes on each side for pink or 8 minutes on each side for more well done.

Prepare the hunter sauce mix according to the directions on the package. Serve with sea salt roasted potatoes (page 21) and steamed green beans.

steamed vegetables

I steam almost all my fresh vegetables: green beans, peas, spinach, corn, carrots, broccoli, snow peas and cauliflower. For a nice touch toss steamed vegetables with butter and slivered almonds.

A steamer can be purchased for a couple of dollars and expands and contracts to fit a variety of pot sizes. To steam, fit a pot with the steamer, and then fill the pot with water to just below the base of the steamer. Bring the water to a boil then add the vegetables. Cover the pot with a tight fitting lid. Turn the heat to low. I like my vegetables a bit crunchy so I find 8 minutes the perfect cooking time. Adjust the cooking time depending on your desired tenderness.

breakfast

scrambled eggs - 34

fried eggs - 35

george's go to hell eggs - 36

breakfast burrito -37

chili omelet - 38

cousin dolan's egg white omelet - 39

eggs benedict - 40

lox and bagels - 42

cousin keith's french toast - 43

pancakes - 44

roll-ups (aka crêpes) - 45

breakfast casserole - 46

home fries - 47

the senator's roast beef hash - 48

sausage gravy and biscuits - 49

creamy grits casserole - 50

pull apart coffee cake - 51

ahhh....there's nothing like waking up to the smell of bacon frying, coffee brewing and toast burning. Bill's dad made breakfast every Sunday morning—he'd make dozens of roll-ups or go through an entire loaf of bread making French toast.

Weekends are for sleeping late then dragging yourself out of bed and having a huge breakfast. Sometimes weekends are for staying out all night then chowing down on bacon, eggs and home fries in the wee hours of the morning at your favorite diner just before crawling onto the couch for a lazy day of recovery, watching sports and napping.

For those of you living in a city the chances are you have your favorite neighborhood coffee shop you frequent for breakfast. When I lived in Manhattan mine was The Viand on 61st and Madison Avenue. It was long and narrow with a counter on the right with seating for about fifteen. There was a row of booths on the left. The aisle between the counter seats and booths was barely wide enough to walk through. Every weekend the diner was packed with at least a thirty-minute wait. I'd frequently go for breakfast with my friends Jenny and Moira and sister Terry. We used to love sitting at the counter watching the short order cook. Every breakfast order, no matter what it was started with a ladle of melted grease poured onto the piping hot griddle. There was always a pile of home fries cooking away in the corner with the cook periodically adding more potatoes, onions and scoops of softened margarine. What great breakfasts, and cheap too!

Many bachelors excel at making breakfast. But for those of you who have yet to scramble your first egg, this chapter starts out with the basics—bacon and eggs. For the rest of you, try something new like the eggs benedict or roast beef hash.

scrambled eggs
serves 1

Scrambled eggs come in a variety of textures. Some folks like them just cooked to a soft, creamy texture, while others like them a little drier, and if you're like my friend Joe, you like them just as they begin to crisp. No matter how you like them the key to successful scrambled eggs is to "keep 'em moving" while you're cooking them. Bill's got it down to a science.

    2 eggs
    splash of milk
    salt and pepper to taste
    2 teaspoons butter

Lightly beat the eggs in a small bowl with the milk, salt and pepper. Melt the butter in a 6-inch skillet over medium heat. Pour in the eggs and with a heat resistant rubber spatula continually move the eggs scraping from the sides and bottom towards the center until desired texture. Remember, "keep 'em moving!"

---

alternatives

If you're fixing scrambled eggs for a crowd for a special occasion use a dozen eggs, and add ⅓ cup fresh herbs such as chopped parsley, chives, tarragon or dill (or a combination of all) when beating the eggs and add ½ cup cream cheese, goat cheese or cheddar cheese just before the eggs have finished cooking.

---

fried eggs

serves 1

Fried eggs are one of those things that you either know how to cook, or you don't. I fall into the "you don't" camp; they either end up like flattened hard boiled eggs, they stick to the pan or I break the yolks. On more than one occasion eggs that started out to be fried ended up scrambled. To minimize the risk of breaking the yolks, cover the skillet with a tight fitting lid. The eggs will cook through without having to flip, thus reducing the risk of broken yolks.

2 eggs
1 tablespoon butter
salt and pepper to taste

Melt the butter in a skillet over medium-high heat until the butter just begins to sizzle. Season with salt and pepper. For sunny side up eggs, cover the pan with a tight fitting lid and cook for about 3 – 4 minutes until the whites are no longer clear but the yolks are still soft.

hints

In addition to sunny side up, fried eggs come in several "over" varieties:

For over easy eggs, flip once and continue to cook for 1 minute so the yolk is still runny.

For over medium, flip once and continue to cook for 2 minutes.

For over hard, flip once and continue to cook until the yolks harden.

eggamuffin

Place a fried egg on a toasted, split English muffin. Break the yolk and mix it around. Top with a slice of cheddar cheese and bacon or sausage and the other half of the English muffin.

george's go to hell eggs
serves 6

This recipe is compliments of our friend George, a former president of the San Diego Bachelor's Club. He featured these eggs at the First Annual Opening Day at Del Mar Race Track Party twelve years ago for thirty guests. This annual party has grown to over four hundred guests. Inevitably someone's girlfriend would ask for eggs "without all the stuff." George's response was, "Go to hell! This ain't Burger King. You get it the way I make it!" Any questions?

5 eggs
2 pound Choriso, cut into bite-sized pieces
1 each red, yellow, green and orange bell pepper, seeded and diced
1 large onion, diced
1 cup sharp cheddar cheese, shredded
6 flour tortillas (6-inch)
salsa (*your favorite brand*)
guacamole (page 16)
salt and pepper to taste

Cook the Choriso, peppers and onions in a large skillet over medium heat for about 5 minutes until the peppers and onions become tender. Beat the eggs slightly; season with salt and pepper and add to the mixture. Continue to cook over medium heat folding the Choriso mixture into the eggs until the eggs are wet but cooked. Add the cheese and continue to fold until the cheese melts. Place a spoonful of the egg mixture on a tortilla; top with salsa and guacamole. Serve home fries (page 47) and Bloody Mary's on the side.

breakfast burrito
makes 2

A few years ago a group of friends were going camping and invited us to join them. I've loved camping ever since I was a kid and Denise had never been. I thought it would be a fun thing to do. We divvied up the meal responsibilities and our friends, Jill and Jennifer, the twins, were in charge of breakfast. They made these ahead of time, wrapped them individually in foil and put them in the cooler. Each morning we put the foil packets over the open campfire to heat up and it made a hearty breakfast before setting out for a day of canoeing.

Spoon the filling onto the left third of the tortilla leaving ¾ of an inch on each side. Fold each side of the tortilla over the mixture and roll up.

2 eggs
2 sausage links, cooked and cut into bite-sized pieces
½ cup sharp cheddar cheese, shredded
1 jalapeno pepper, seeded and diced
salsa (*your favorite brand*)
2 flour tortillas (6-inch)

Scramble the eggs according to the instructions on page 34, mixing in the sausage pieces as the eggs are cooking.

To prepare the tortillas spoon the egg and sausage mixture onto the tortilla. Top with cheese, jalapeno and salsa. Fold the tortilla as described above.

chili omelet

serves 1

There's nothing like this hearty omelet to carry you through the day. It's a meal in itself. The key to making a successful omelet is to work quickly and to keep the eggs moving. Don't limit yourself to just a chili omelet. Get creative and use your favorite foods for fillings.

2 eggs
splash of milk
dash of salt and pepper
1 tablespoon butter
½ cup Billy's chili (*page 14*)
¼ cup grated cheddar cheese
1 jalapeno pepper, diced
Tabasco to taste

Beat the eggs lightly in a small bowl with the milk, salt and pepper until slightly beaten. Heat the chili in a small saucepan over low - medium heat. Melt the butter in a 6-inch skillet over medium-high heat until it begins to foam and sizzle. Pour in the eggs and lightly shake the pan in a forward and backward motion. As soon as the edges of the eggs begin to cook, using a heat resistant rubber spatula, gently push the edges of the eggs slightly towards the center of the pan, then tilt the skillet to allow the uncooked eggs in the center to flow around to the sides of the pan. Continue this process until the eggs are almost fully cooked. It should be just about one minute from the time you pour the eggs into the pan.

Add the heated chili, cheddar cheese and jalapenos to one half of the omelet. Fold the other half of the omelet over the filling. Cook for 30 – 45 seconds until the cheese begins to melt. Slide out onto a plate. Serve with home fries (page 47).

cousin dolan's egg white omelet

My cousin Dolan is the most fit and disciplined person I know. He's religious about working out *every single day* and is rarely tempted by sinful foods.

We had a big family breakfast a few weeks ago. Some of the cousins came over the day after the 27th Annual Sullivan Family Christmas party (because we hadn't seen enough of each other the night before!) The breakfast was no fuss, which meant no special orders. Upon leaving the family party at 1:30 am, Dolan requested an egg white omelet—a special order.

The following morning the cousins trickled in. Susan prepped the eggs, setting aside egg whites for Dolan. Keith took the French toast station, Bill was on home fries and I was on bacon and sausage. Uncle John and Aunt Loretta kept the coffee cups filled; Mom, sister Missy and Cousin Dawn made sure the serving table was in order, while Susie and Sarah provided colorful commentary on the party the night before. Jack kept the fire going, while Matthew kept the Christmas music playing. My dad did what he does best— he stayed out of the kitchen. When we were ready to eat, there were egg whites, but no Dolan. When we were finished eating, there were egg whites, but no Dolan, the cousin with the special order. Suddenly, there was a knock at the door; finally it was Cousin Dolan with his three adorable kids Patrick, Sean and Annie. Dolan whipped up a healthy egg white omelet. He put us all to shame as we loosened our belts.

Everyone critiqued the manuscript of this book. Uncle John contributed his tuna melt, the French toast was renamed Cousin Keith's French toast; in order not to leave Dolan out of the fun, we added his egg white omelet.

For a healthier omelet use three egg whites, and fill with your favorite fillings.

eggs benedict
serves 1

When I think of Sunday brunch, I think of eggs benedict at the original Clyde's restaurant in Georgetown. During my college days, many Sundays were spent rolling out of bed at about noon and heading over to Clyde's on M Street in Georgetown for the hair of the dog and brunch. Eggs benedict was a popular brunch item.

Unless you're really ambitious and want to make your own hollandaise sauce, I recommend using McCormick brand. It tastes just like homemade.

2 slices Canadian bacon
2 eggs
water
2 tablespoons white vinegar (optional)
1 package McCormick Hollandaise Sauce Mix
4 tablespoons butter
English muffin, split and toasted
black truffles, optional

Fry the Canadian bacon over medium heat until it's brown on both sides.

Fill a medium saucepan halfway with water. Add the vinegar (the vinegar helps the eggs to coagulate when they hit the water) and bring to a simmer over medium heat.

While the water is heating, prepare the hollandaise sauce according the directions on the package.

When the water in the pan simmers, break the eggs into the pan being careful not to break the yolks. Cook in the simmering water for about 4 – 5 minutes until the eggs whites are no longer translucent.

To serve, place the split English muffins on a plate. Top each half with a slice of Canadian bacon and an egg. Pour hollandaise sauce over the eggs and sprinkle with truffles. Voila! A terrific Sunday brunch.

alternatives

Try substituting smoked salmon for the Canadian bacon and add a few capers and chopped onions for garnish on top of the hollandaise sauce.

poor man's eggs benedict

Thanks to my friend Jimmy, there's a "poor man's" version of eggs benedict. Substitute ½ cup Campbell's Cheddar Cheese Soup, heated for the hollandaise sauce. Omit the truffles (they're not for the budget conscious).

lox and bagels
serves 4

Fresh lox thinly sliced with all the toppings served with fresh bagels makes a great nosh. It is a real treat as a breakfast meal or part of a full fare brunch.

8 ounces smoked salmon, thinly sliced
4 fresh bagels, sliced in half
8 ounce package cream cheese
1 egg white, hard boiled, finely diced
¼ red onion, finely diced
3 tablespoons capers
lemon wedges

Lay salmon on a serving on a tray. Garnish the tray with cream cheese, diced egg white, cream cheese, onions and capers.

Allow your guests to assemble their own bagels to their liking. Serve with mimosas or Bloody Mary's.

hard boiled eggs

Place eggs in a saucepan filled with cold water. Bring to a boil. Reduce the heat to low and simmer for 15 minutes. Remove eggs and place in a bowl of cold water. This makes them easier to peel.

For soft boiled eggs, bring water to a simmer first, then gently place the eggs in the water (it's helpful to place one egg at a time on a tablespoon and lower it into the water to avoid cracking). Simmer for 3 – 4 minutes. Remove from water and serve.

cousin keith's french toast

serves 2

Don't you just love the taste of salty bacon or sausage mixed with sweet maple syrup? French toast, crispy on the outside and warm and soft on the inside, served with butter, maple syrup and crunchy bacon satisfies the desire for sweet, salty, crispy and soft all at the same time.

2 eggs slightly beaten
1 tablespoon milk
½ teaspoon sugar
¼ teaspoon cinnamon
4 slices semi-stale white bread
4 tablespoons butter
powdered sugar
maple syrup

Lightly beat the eggs, milk and sugar together. Pour into a shallow dish. Dip the bread into the egg mixture coating both sides.

Melt 1 tablespoon of butter over medium–high heat in a large skillet. When the butter begins to sizzle add the bread. Sprinkle with cinnamon. Cook for 2 – 3 minutes until it's nicely browned, then flip and sprinkle with cinnamon. Cook for another 2 – 3 minutes. Remove from pan; sprinkle with powdered sugar. Top with soft butter and syrup. Serve with bacon or sausage.

suggestions

If you're making French toast for a crowd, keep the cooked pieces warm in an 250° oven. Dress up by slicing on a diagonal, arranging on a platter and add sliced strawberries, peaches or bananas on top.

holiday french toast

Mix ½ teaspoon nutmeg into 2 tablespoons of eggnog (available in the refrigerator section of your grocer during the holiday season). Omit the milk, sugar and cinnamon. Prepare according to the directions on the left. Sprinkle with nutmeg.

pancakes

makes 8 pancakes

What can I say? Pancakes don't need an introduction. They are *the* classic all-American breakfast. There is nothing wrong with using packaged pancake mix but the fresh batter below is just as easy to whip up.

1 egg
1 cup milk
2 tablespoons butter, melted
1 cup flour
2 teaspoons baking powder
2 tablespoons sugar
6 tablespoons butter (for cooking & serving)
maple syrup

---

bacon and sausage

Cooking bacon and sausage over lower heat prevents it from cooking too quickly and burning.

Place bacon or sausage links or patties in a skillet. Cook over low-medium heat turning once for about 15 minutes or until browned.

Remove from the pan and place on a plate lined with paper towels to drain excess grease.

Beat the egg, milk and butter in a medium bowl. In a separate bowl mix the flour, baking powder and sugar together; then add to the milk mixture, stirring just enough to blend together (it's okay to have a few lumps in the batter).

Melt enough butter in a large skillet over medium heat to lightly coat the bottom. When the butter begins to foam and sizzle pour in about ¼ cup of batter for each pancake. When bubbles form in the pancakes they are ready to flip and should do so easily with a spatula. Flip and cook on the other side for about a minute until nicely browned. Serve stacked and top with melted butter and syrup and bacon or sausage as a side.

roll-ups (aka crêpes)
serves 4

Roll-ups were a Medved family favorite. They'd eat them by the dozen after Sunday Mass.

1½ cups milk
1 cup flour
2 eggs
1 tablespoon vegetable oil
⅛ teaspoon salt
4 tablespoons butter
grape jelly, strawberry jam or apple butter for filling
powdered sugar

Combine all ingredients in a bowl and beat until well mixed into a consistent batter. Melt enough butter in a 6-inch skillet over medium heat to completely cover the bottom. When the butter begins to sizzle remove from heat and pour in two tablespoons of the batter. Tilt the skillet to thinly spread the batter to cover the bottom. You only want a thin film of batter lining the skillet, so pour any excess back into the batter bowl. Cook over medium heat until the edges begin to pull away from the pan. Turn the crêpe and cook on the other side for about a minute until nicely browned. Place filling on crêpe and roll up. Sprinkle with powdered sugar.

breakfast casserole
serves 8

This is a great dish for several reasons—it can be made ahead of time, it serves a crowd, is a complete meal in itself and it's really easy!

1 pound sausage roll (*I prefer Jimmy Dean*)
6 slices white bread
6 eggs
2 cups milk
1½ cups grated cheddar cheese
salt and pepper to taste
dash of cayenne pepper

Crumble sausage in a skillet and cook 10 – 15 minutes over medium heat until browned. Pour out the grease and set aside.

Place the bread in a 9 x 12-inch baking dish.

Beat eggs with milk, salt, pepper, and cayenne pepper until well beaten. Stir in the cheese.

Sprinkle the sausage over the bread then pour the egg mixture over the bread. Cover and refrigerate overnight.

When ready to bake, preheat the oven to 350° and bake for 40 – 45 minutes. Cut into squares to serve. Accompany with cut-up fresh fruit such as strawberries, oranges, bananas, melon or pineapple.

home fries
serves 2

2 large potatoes, peeled, quartered and thinly sliced
4 tablespoons butter
1 onion, halved and thinly sliced
¼ teaspoon paprika
¼ teaspoon garlic powder
salt and pepper to taste
cayenne pepper to taste

Melt the butter in a large skillet pan over medium heat. Add the potatoes, onion, paprika, garlic powder, salt, pepper and cayenne pepper and mix together. Cook for 15 minutes until soft. Turn the potatoes adding more seasoning and butter, if necessary, and cook for 15 minutes. Turn periodically until potatoes are brown and crispy all over being careful not to burn.

hint

To prepare in advance, boil the peeled, quartered potatoes for 15 minutes in salted water. Cool, then slice. Refrigerate until ready to use.

If you plan to peel and/or slice raw potatoes in advance, place in a bowl of cold water to prevent them from turning gray/brown.

Orelda's Country Style Hash Browns Shredded Potato (found in the frozen food section) is an excellent alternative if you don't want to peel and slice fresh potatoes.

the senator's roast beef hash
serves 2

My friend Lowell Weicker (or as I call him, "The Senator" because he was the Senator from Connecticut when I interned for him during college) contributed his famous bourbon hot dog recipe to *the tiny kitchen cooking and entertaining* and it was a hit! He wanted to contribute to this book as well. During his intermittent bachelor days he says he did just fine fending for himself in the kitchen. One of his breakfast favorites is roast beef hash. I've only had corned beef hash, but he swears this is much better and insists you use canned roast beef hash.

The Senator and his wife Claudia are excellent cooks and very gracious hosts.

1 can (15 ounces) roast beef hash (*The Senator prefers Mary Kitchen*)
1 potato, peeled and diced
1 onion, diced
4 tablespoons butter

Melt the butter in a large skillet over medium heat. Add the potatoes and onions and cook for 15 minutes until tender.

Mix the roast beef hash into the potato and onion mixture. Continue cooking and mixing for about 10 minutes until well browned.

> ### corned beef hash
> Used left over corned beef from page 95 instead of the roast beef. Try serving hash over toast topped with poached or fried eggs.

sausage gravy and biscuits
serves 4

1 pound sausage roll (*I prefer Jimmy Dean*)
1 teaspoon sage (optional)
dash of cayenne pepper (optional)
4 tablespoons flour
2 cups milk
1 can biscuits *(I prefer Pillsbury)*

Crumble the sausage into the skillet and add the sage and cayenne pepper. Cook over medium heat, stirring occasionally until the sausage is well browned. Transfer the sausage to a bowl while making the gravy. Do not discard the drippings.

To make the gravy remove the skillet from the heat and add flour to the drippings until well blended into a paste consistency.

Return the skillet to the heat and gradually add the milk, stirring constantly. Cook over medium heat until the gravy thickens. Return the sausage to the gravy and mix well.

Prepare the biscuits according to the directions on the package.

To serve, split the biscuits in half and smother with sausage gravy.

creamy grits casserole
serves lots

You don't have to be southern to enjoy grits. If you have never tried them I encourage you to do so. They're a great dish for a brunch.

1 cup hominy grits
3 cups milk
1 teaspoon salt
¼ teaspoon pepper
2 eggs, lightly beaten
1 cup water
4 tablespoons butter
1 cup cheddar cheese, shredded
1 tablespoon Worcestershire
Tabasco to taste

Preheat the oven to 350°.

Mix the grits, milk, salt and pepper in a saucepan over medium heat. Cook, stirring frequently until the mixture is thick, approximately 5 minutes. Remove from heat. Add the eggs and water and mix thoroughly. Return to heat and cook until the mixture thickens again, approximately 5 – 10 minutes. Stir in the butter, cheese, Worcestershire and Tabasco. Pour into a 9 x 12-inch greased baking dish. Bake for 30 minutes.

pull apart coffee cake
serves lots

This coffee cake is fantastic! Not only do you get the aroma of freshly baked bread but you also get to savor the irresistible smell of cinnamon; it's addictive. The nice thing about this is it can be prepared in just minutes the night before.

   1 package (24 per package) frozen dinner rolls dough (*I prefer Richs brand*)
   ½ cup chopped pecans
   ¾ cup brown sugar
   1 teaspoon cinnamon
   1 package (3.5 ounces) vanilla pudding mix (*not instant; and keep it dry!*)
   6 tablespoons butter

Thaw the package of dinner rolls dough (approximately 30 minutes). Lightly grease a tube pan with butter and sprinkle the bottom with pecans. Place the rolls tightly together in the pan covering the bottom, then layer pecans and rolls as necessary using the remaining rolls.

   Mix together brown sugar, cinnamon, and dry pudding mix and sprinkle the mixture liberally over the rolls. Dot the top of the rolls with butter. Cover with foil and let stand overnight.

   When ready to bake preheat oven to 350°. Bake for 20 – 25 minutes. Let cool for 5 minutes, then turn out upside down on a plate. The top of the coffee cake is crusted with pecans and the pudding mixture melts between all the rolls. Serve warm and let your guests indulge by pulling the rolls apart. Have napkins ready!

sandwiches, soups & salads

uncle john's tuna melt - 54

bill's tuna fish salad - 54

grilled cheese sandwich - 55

reuben - 56

classic club sandwich - 57

cheesesteak sub - 58

dad's bronx deli - 67

chicken noodle soup - 68

tomato soup - 69

french onion soup - 70

salad niçoise - 72

cobb salad - 73

nothing says lunch like a sandwich on fresh bread served with ruffled potato chips, a crispy cold dill pickle and an ice-cold Coke. My personal favorite is a club sandwich. The tuna fish salad sandwich, however, is probably the most popular all-American sandwich. I don't care for tuna fish salad because I was "overtunaed" as a kid growing up in a Catholic family. Every Friday I was served (*served*, but didn't necessarily eat) tuna fish salad—for lunch at school, then again for dinner. At school they'd load a pile of tuna fish (dark meat, of course) into a split hot dog bun, topped off with a half-slice of American cheese, cut on the diagonal, and they called it a "Tuna Boat." No matter how it was served, it was *still* tuna fish! Chances are you have a can of tuna in your cupboard now.

As a bachelor, Bill never ran short. From time to time as the several cans in the cupboard were reaching their "best if eaten by" date I would suggest to Bill he either eat the tuna fish or throw it away. I knew I was never going to eat it and in all the years I had known him I had never, *ever*, seen him eat tuna. He insisted we keep it and that he'd eat it someday. Well, someday finally came when I decided to make it for him for dinner one night (before the "best if eaten by" date arrived). I made tuna fish salad for him, while I made myself a beautiful, thick, juicy filet mignon with béarnaise sauce and baked potato. Needless to say it didn't go over too well with Bill, but I was laughing hysterically! That tuna and the other cans went in the garbage that night. Occasionally, canned tuna makes it back into the pantry and Bill swears he really does eat it! Guys, if your girlfriend suggests something that's been hanging around in your refrigerator or cupboard for a while be pitched; listen to her or you might get "tunafished" too!

No sandwich is complete without the accompaniment of a dill pickle. Bill keeps a jar of dill pickles in the refrigerator and spices them up by adding a chopped habanero pepper to the jar.

uncle john's tuna melt
makes 1

Even though I was "overtunaed" as a child (see page 53) I won't deny you the pleasure of tuna fish recipes.

1 can (6 ounces) white meat tuna
¾ teaspoon thyme
1 tablespoon minced onion
1 teaspoon capers
2 tablespoons mayonnaise
salt and pepper to taste
1 pita bread (6-inch), cut in half
2 slices cheddar cheese

Preheat the broiler.

    In a small bowl mix together tuna, thyme, onion, capers, mayonnaise, salt and pepper. Place a scoop of tuna on each half of the pita. Top with cheddar cheese. Place under the broiler until the cheese melts, about 1 minute.

---

bill's tuna fish salad

1 can (6 ounces) white meat tuna
1 stalk celery, diced
2 tablespoons minced onion
2 tablespoons shredded carrots
1 teaspoon sweet relish
2 tablespoons mayonnaise
salt and pepper to taste
1 lettuce leaf
2 tomato slices
2 slices white bread

In a small bowl mix together tuna, celery, onion, carrots, mayonnaise, salt and pepper. Spread tuna fish salad on a slice of bread. Top with lettuce, tomato and the other slice of bread. Serve with a dill pickle and chips.

grilled cheese sandwich
makes 1 sandwich

Sometimes you just feel like something sinfully greasy. This is it. There's nothing like a buttery, crispy on the outside, gooey on the inside grilled cheese sandwich. It's even better when it's served with a cup of tomato soup.

2 slices white bread
2 slices American cheese
2 tablespoons butter

Melt the butter in a skillet over low to medium heat. Once the butter is melted, place one slice of bread in the skillet. Top with the cheese then the second slice of bread. Brown the sandwich for 3 – 4 minutes, flip and brown on the other side for 3 – 4 minutes. Watch carefully so you don't burn it.

alternative serving suggestions

Try doctoring up the basic grilled cheese sandwich by adding ham, bacon and/or tomato.

When I was an intern on Capitol Hill I used to get lunch every day for the Senator's appointment secretary, Cindy. I'd get her grilled Swiss cheese and bacon on rye bread. It was delicious. Try it.

reuben

makes 1 sandwich

A reuben is one of those sandwiches people never fix at home—who knows why. Maybe because it's so messy. Whenever I see one served at a restaurant it looks so good I wish I liked corned beef, sauerkraut and Russian dressing.

2 slices corned beef
2 slices Swiss cheese
2 slices rye bread
2 tablespoons butter
1 can (14.5 ounces) sauerkraut
Russian dressing *(I prefer Ken's brand)*

open faced reuben

For a less messy sandwich try an open faced reuben. Preheat the broiler. Place bread on a sheet of aluminum foil. Top each slice with corned beef, sauerkraut and Swiss cheese. Broil for 3 – 4 minutes until the cheese melts. Smother the sandwich with Russian dressing. Eat open faced with fork and knife.

Melt the butter in a frying pan over low to medium heat. Once the butter is melted, place one slice of rye bread in the pan. Top with corned beef, Swiss cheese, sauerkraut and Russian dressing then the second slice of bread. Brown the sandwich for 3 – 4 minutes, flip and brown on the other side for 3 – 4 minutes. Watch carefully so you don't burn it.

classic club sandwich
makes 1 sandwich

This is my all time favorite sandwich. It reminds me of when I was a kid. On special occasions when we'd go out to lunch, or if we were travelling and staying at a hotel I would order a club sandwich served with ruffled potato chips, a dill pickle and a Shirley Temple. I loved the frilly tooth picks stuck into each of the triangular quarters of the sandwich. To this day, whenever I travel and stay at a hotel I order a club sandwich.

3 slices white bread, lightly toasted
3 slices turkey or chicken
3 strips bacon, cooked
2 lettuce leaves
1 tomato, sliced
mayonnaise
frilly toothpicks (optional)

classic blt

The classic BLT is a club sandwich minus the turkey and one slice of toast. Or, you could say the classic club sandwich is the classic BLT with turkey and another slice of toast.

Spread each piece of toast with mayonnaise. Place the turkey and bacon on one slice; top with another slice of toast. Place the lettuce and tomato and top with the other slice of toast. Cut on the diagonal in each direction to create triangular quarters. Place a frilly toothpick in each quarter. Serve with potato chips and a dill pickle.

cheesesteak sub

makes 1 sandwich

This is a really good gooey sandwich and is a great way to use leftover steak.

- ½ tablespoon olive oil
- ½ onion, thinly sliced
- ½ green pepper, seeded and thinly sliced
- 3 ounces steak or roast beef, sliced very thin
- 2 slices Swiss cheese
- 1 sub roll

Heat the olive oil in a skillet over medium heat. Sauté the onion and green pepper slices about 3 minutes until tender. Keep them moving so they don't burn. Add the steak and toss together. Cook for about 5 minutes until the steak begins to brown. Add the cheese and continue to toss the mixture until the cheese melts. Keep it moving so the cheese doesn't stick to the pan and burn.

Place in the split sub roll. Enjoy!

french onion soup

reuben sandwich

shrimp kebabs

broiled salmon

roasted chicken

barbecued ribs

cocktail

dad's bronx deli
makes 1 sandwich

My dad grew up in a Bronx neighborhood of Irish immigrant families. The standard cold cuts were bologna, liverwurst and Swiss cheese. He wasn't aware of traditional cold cuts such as roast beef, ham and turkey until he went to West Point. Until he met my mother there was plenty he was not aware of, not the least of which were cheeses such as brie and camembert. He thought cheeses were limited to Swiss, American and cream cheese. My father often wonders how he made it through his first nineteen years without my mother!

My dad doesn't really cook or do much in terms of food preparation. Every once in a while he'll go to the commissary and bring home the Bronx deli fixins.

2 slices bologna
2 slices liverwurst
2 slices Swiss cheese
2 slices rye bread
mayonnaise

Spread mayonnaise on the bread. Layer the bologna, liverwurst and Swiss cheese. Top with the second slice of bread. Serve with potato chips and dill pickle.

chicken noodle soup
serves 4

Chicken noodle soup is an old-fashioned comfort food and there are certain times when I just have to have it and nothing else will do. I have tried repeatedly to make a great, flavorful, clear chicken broth that doesn't take a lot of time or effort. Then I discovered Swanson Chicken Broth available in the canned food section. It is so good and tastes just like homemade it's not worth the effort for me to make it from scratch. This is a great way to use left over chicken.

  1 tablespoon olive oil
  1 cup sliced baby carrots
  1 cup diced celery
  1 medium onion or shallot, diced
  5 cups chicken broth (*I prefer Swanson Chicken Broth*)
  2 tablespoons fresh parsley, chopped
  1 cup cooked chicken, cut into ½-inch cubes
  1 cup cooked spaghetti, cut into 1-inch pieces

Heat the olive oil in a stockpot over medium heat. Add the carrots, celery and onion and cook for 5 minutes or until tender. Do not let them brown. Add the chicken broth, parsley, cooked chicken and cooked spaghetti to the chicken broth. Heat over high heat until it simmers. Serve piping hot!

tomato soup

serves 4

This is a really good, rich soup, almost bordering on a sauce. It is so easy to make and gets rave reviews.

    2 tablespoons olive oil
    1 shallot, minced
    1 garlic clove, minced
    1 can (28 ounces) crushed tomatoes or tomato purée
    2 cups chicken broth
    3 tablespoons butter
    ½ to 1 cup heavy cream (depending on how rich you like it)
    3 tablespoons fresh basil, chopped
    fresh ground black pepper to taste

Heat the olive oil in a stockpot over medium heat. Sauté the shallot and garlic for 1 – 2 minutes. Add the crushed tomatoes or tomato purée and the chicken broth. Simmer for 30 minutes. The soup will begin to thicken. Add the butter one tablespoon at a time stirring continuously. Stir in cream and basil and heat through. Season with fresh ground black pepper.

french onion soup
serves 4

In November 1992 I was working for a company that was going through hard times. One day they re-orged half of the company right out of jobs. Karen, Joan and I suddenly joined the ranks of the unemployed and decided to take off until after the holidays. We started the Wednesday Lunch Club, and took turns hosting lunch at our apartments. When we went to Karen's she served French onion soup, Caesar salad, garlic bread and lots of wine. French onion soup will forever remind me of the Wednesday Lunch Club.

The soup is rich and flavorful. The slow cooking of the onions brings out their natural sugars. The diversity of the textures is pleasing: crispy, but gooey cheese on the top and slightly crunchy onions.

2 tablespoons butter
2 tablespoons olive oil
2 large *sweet* onions, peeled, halved and finely sliced
1 teaspoon thyme
¼ teaspoon salt
½ teaspoon sugar
6 cups beef broth (*I prefer Swanson Beef Broth*)
¼ cup white wine
freshly ground black pepper to taste
4 slices French bread cut into 1-inch slices and lightly toasted
2 ½ cups Gruyère or Emmentaler cheese, shredded

Heat butter and olive oil in a large saucepan over medium heat. When the butter melts and bubbles, add the onions, thyme and salt and mix together. Cook for 5 minutes until the onions are translucent and tender.

Reduce the heat to low, cover and cook for 15 minutes, stirring occasionally until the onions turn a golden brown. Uncover, stir in the sugar, raise the heat to medium and cook uncovered for 30 minutes, stirring frequently until the onions turn a rich, dark brown and begin to caramelize.

Stir in the beef broth, wine and pepper and scrape any crystallized juices from the bottom of the pan. Bring the soup to a boil. Reduce the heat to low, cover and simmer for 10 minutes.

To assemble the soup

Preheat the oven to 400°.

Arrange individual ovenproof serving crocks or mugs on a baking sheet. Place a slice of French bread in the bottom of each crock. Top each with a tablespoon of cheese. Ladle the soup into each crock and top each with the remaining cheese.

Place the cookie sheet in the oven and bake for 15 minutes until the cheese is crisp, bubbly and golden brown.

alternative serving suggestion

Instead of preparing the soup in individual bowls, prepare in one large, ovenproof soup tureen or bowl with a rim. It's quite impressive looking. Let your guests serve themselves.

salad niçoise

serves 2

This traditional Mediterranean salad has become quite popular in trendy American restaurants. It's so easy to assemble and creates quite a colorful dish.

6 ounces fresh tuna, grilled and sliced

4 cups mixed salad greens

8 small, new red potatoes, boiled (see page 19 for boiling potatoes), quartered and chilled

½ cup green beans, trimmed, blanched and chilled

¼ red onion, thinly sliced

8 small black olives

1 hard-boiled egg, quartered lengthwise

½ cup Newman's Own Olive Oil and Vinegar Dressing

Place the salad greens, potatoes, green beans, onions and olives in a bowl. Add the dressing and toss gently. Place a mound of salad on each plate. Top with the tuna and garnish with hard boiled egg.

what are blanched green beans?

Blanching is a cooking method whereby fruits or vegetables are cooked in boiling water for a very short time (a few seconds up to a minute, depending on the food, yielding a tender texture) then immediately submerged into ice water to stop the cooking and preserve the color.

To blanch green beans place in boiling water for 1 minute; remove immediately and transfer to a bowl of ice water. Let stand in the ice water for 10 minutes. Refrigerate until ready to use.

cobb salad

serves 2

This is a great salad to prepare for your girlfriend for lunch on a hot summer afternoon.

4 cups mixed salad greens
2 cups cooked chicken or turkey, cut into ¾-inch cubes
1 ripe avocado, cut into ¾-inch cubes
1 large tomato, diced
8 strips bacon, cooked and crumbled
4 ounces bleu cheese, crumbled
2 eggs, hard-boiled and chopped
Newman's Own Balsamic Vinaigrette

Place a bed of salad greens on each plate. To impress your lunch guest, "decorate" each plate by arranging the remaining ingredients in rows next to each other. Starting from the left side of the plate and working your way to the right arrange as follows: avocado, tomato, chicken, bleu cheese, eggs then bacon. Drizzle the top with salad dressing.

snacks

tacos with all the fixins - 76

macho nachos - 77

chili con queso - 78

chicken wings - 79

mini shrimp kebabs - 80

dad's bronx appetizer - 81

pizza - 82

hot crab dip - 83

stuffed mushrooms - 84

bill's famous bacon and horseradish dip - 85

mr. p's smoky pecans - 86

spiced shrimp - 87

grills with - 88

drunken melon - 89

What guy doesn't like to sit around on weekends and watch football, college hoops, golf, baseball, hockey or NASCAR? Or any sport for that matter. I do. I love having my "Saturday Afternoon Beer" along with a few snacks after doing yard work.

Before I met Denise, I worked at EDS in the Motor Sports Division. I was in charge of the Indy Timing and Scoring System, went to all the races and it was then I got hooked on Indy Car racing. After several years I left the Motor Sports Division but was and am still a die hard Indy Car fan. I came up with a tradition I still carry on to this day. Each year on the last Sunday in May I fix myself my favorite snacks, park a cooler of beer right next to me, put the TV out on the patio and settle in for the five hour Indianapolis 500. My menu includes macho nachos, chicken wings and chili (of course).

I love the building process involved in making nachos. Everyone has their own construction style with the nachos—layered neatly, carefully arranging the toppings or randomly piling all ingredients on top in a heap. Nachos are the perfect snack whether you're just off the ski slopes or sitting around idly watching a game. It's kind of a bonding thing—pulling apart the pile of chips with the gooey cheese and toppings falling all over the place.

Another favorite snack of mine is chicken wings. The hotter, the better. I resurrected my bacon and horseradish dip for this book. I hadn't made it in years—in fact I forgot about it. I used to make it all the time when I was in college and right out of college. It's cheap and everyone loves it, especially when served with ruffled potato chips.

Enjoy your snacks!

tacos with all the fixins'

serves 2

Bill has to eat Mexican food at least once a week or experiences withdrawal symptoms. His favorite fast food restaurant is Taco Bell (or Taco Swell as my brother-in-law Bob refers to it). Tacos are a great snack, quick and easy to prepare.

1 pound ground beef
1 package taco seasoning mix *(I prefer Old El Paso brand low sodium)*
1 cup cheddar cheese, shredded
1 tomato, diced
¼ head lettuce, chopped
2 jalapenos, chopped
guacamole (page 16)
sour cream
6 hard taco shells (or soft flour tortillas)

Preheat the oven to 375°.

Cook ground beef in a skillet over medium heat for about 10 minutes or until browned. Prepare the taco seasoning according to the directions on the package.

Place the taco shells on a baking sheet and heat in oven for approximately 5 minutes. Keep an eye on them—they burn quickly.

Fill the shells with seasoned meat and top with cheese, tomatoes, lettuce, jalapenos, guacamole and sour cream. Serve with ice cold Coronas!

macho nachos
serves 6 - 8

When we snack on tortilla chips and salsa, Bill carefully selects the unbroken ones and preserves them for when he makes nachos. If I try to snatch a whole one he snatches it back.

    2 pounds ground beef
    2 packages taco seasoning mix *(I prefer Old El Paso)*
    1 bag (13.5 ounces) tortilla chips *(I prefer Tostitos)*
    2 cups shredded cheddar cheese or pre-mixed Mexican cheese blend
    6 fresh jalapeno peppers, diced
    1 container (8 ounces) sour cream
    guacamole (page 16)
    1 jar (16 ounces) salsa *(Bill prefers Chi-Chi's hot style)*

Remove upper rack and preheat oven to 350°.
   Prepare a double recipe of taco meat according to the directions on page 76.
   To assemble the nachos, line either a cookie sheet, pizza pan or other large flat pan with aluminum foil (it makes cleanup so much easier). Place a layer of tortilla chips (be generous and let the chips overlap) and sprinkle meat liberally over the chips. Top with jalapenos then cheese. Add another layer of chips, meat, jalapenos and cheese. Continue to layer until all ingredients have been used. You will end up with a pyramid shape. The top layer should be generously covered with cheese and sprinkled with jalapenos. Place pan on the bottom rack of the oven. Bake for approximately 5 minutes until the cheese melts. Watch it carefully so the chips

don't burn.

To serve, top liberally with large spoonfuls of sour cream, guacamole and salsa. It's quite colorful.

---

alternative serving suggestions

For additional color and flavor add black olives, chopped onions, chopped scallions, or chopped green or red peppers.

For the vegetarian nacho lover, just omit the taco meat.

chili con queso

2 cups Billy's Chili (page 14)
1 package (16 ounces) Velveeta cheese
cayenne pepper to taste
tortilla chips

Combine chili, cheese and cayenne in a saucepan over medium heat. Mix together. Heat until cheese melts and chili and cheese are well blended, stirring occasionally. Serve warm with tortilla chips for dipping.

---

chicken wings

serves 4

Okay, so no one makes wings quite like Hooter's, but these are pretty darn good! While frozen chicken wings are available and good to use, try buying fresh chicken wings. For a healthier version, use white meat chicken strips instead of wings.

2 pounds chicken wings
1 cup hot wing sauce *(Bill prefers Crystal)*
6 stalks celery, cut into 3-inch slices
Blue cheese or ranch dressing (*I prefer Ken's*)

Preheat the oven to 350°.

Drench wings in hot sauce until the wings are thoroughly coated. Place wings on a cookie sheet lined with aluminum foil. Bake for 5 minutes. Turn wings. Apply more hot sauce to the wings with a pastry brush or spoon. Bake for another 5 minutes, turn and add more hot sauce. To crisp the wings, turn the oven to broil and broil for 5 minutes on each side, adding more sauce.

To serve, transfer the wings to a serving dish and accompany with sliced celery and bleu cheese or ranch dressing and lots of napkins.

alternative

For extra crispy wings, fry them first. Heat ½ cup vegetable oil in a large skillet over medium heat. When the oil starts to sizzle, add the drenched wings and cook about 10 minutes until browned on all sides, turning occasionally. Remove from oil, drain on paper towel, then place on cookie sheet and proceed as described above.

For a grilled flavor, grill over hot coals.

mini shrimp kebabs
serves 4

These are great little one-bite appetizers. They look really great, like you fussed all day! See the mouth-watering picture in the middle of the book.

12 large shrimp, shells removed (but not the tails)
2 scallions, cut into 1½-inch pieces, light green and white parts only
½ *each* red bell pepper and yellow bell pepper, cut into 1 x 1-inch pieces
½ cup of Newman's Own Olive Oil and Vinegar Dressing
12 bamboo skewers (6-inch)

Soak the bamboo skewers in cold water for 30 minutes. This will prevent them from burning and breaking.

Marinate the shrimp in Newman's Own Olive Oil and Vinegar Dressing in a Ziploc bag in the refrigerator for 30 minutes.

To assemble the kebabs, place a piece of pepper followed by a piece of scallion, shrimp and another piece of pepper on each skewer.

Preheat the broiler.

Place the assembled skewers on a broiler pan. Broil for 2 minutes per side. Remove from broiler.

dad's bronx appetizer
serves 1

This recipe is compliments of my father. Like the Bronx Deli (page 67) this was a favorite of his growing up in the Bronx and is somewhat nostalgic for him. My dad doesn't do much in the kitchen but from time to time he'll fix himself a Bronx appetizer plate, plop in front of the TV and indulge.

1 can (3.75 ounces) sardines (*my dad prefers King Oscar*)
4 ounces salami, sliced
4 ounces Swiss cheese, sliced
saltine crackers

Drain and rinse the sardines. Assemble ingredients in any order you like. Wash down with a cold beer or beverage of your choice.

pizza

makes 4 pizzas

My friend Steve gave me this recipe for homemade pizza sauce and it is superb! It doesn't take long to whip it up. If you don't have the time or ingredients handy, try Contadina Pizza Quick Sauce. It's a great substitute.

Pizza made with pita is "less filling and tastes great" (sound familiar?) and has fewer carbs than some doughier crusts. Plus, the crust crisps nicely.

Make several ahead of time and freeze (hint: the large pitas, 11-inch, fit in a Ziploc gallon bag; the small pitas, 6-inch, fit in a Ziploc sandwich bag).

1 can (10.7 ounces) tomato puree
1 teaspoon garlic powder
1 tablespoon oregano
½ teaspoon sugar
½ cup Parmesan cheese, shredded
½ cup Romano cheese, shredded
olive oil
4 large pitas (11-inch)
your favorite toppings

Preheat the oven to 450°.

To make the sauce, mix tomato puree, garlic powder, oregano and sugar together.

To prepare a pizza, lightly brush a pita with olive oil on both sides. Spoon pizza sauce over the pita. Sprinkle with cheeses. Place prepared pizza on a piece of aluminum foil and place in the oven. Bake for 15 minutes until the cheese melts.

hot crab dip

serves 6

Growing up near the Maryland shoreline, crabs are a local favorite. Pickin' crabs can be fun but it's definitely one of those things you (and everyone with you) has to be in the mood for. It's a lot of work, is messy and you really have to work for your food. Crab dip is a great way to enjoy crab without all the work or mess. Buy pre-picked crab meat in a package for this recipe.

8 ounces lump crab meat
½ cup mayonnaise
1 package (3 ounces) cream cheese, softened
2 tablespoons lemon juice
½ onion, finely diced
1 tablespoon chopped chives or scallions
1 tablespoon lemon juice
1 teaspoon horseradish
dash of cayenne pepper
Tabasco to taste
Ritz crackers

Preheat the oven to 350°.

Mix mayonnaise, cream cheese and lemon juice until smooth. Stir in remaining ingredients (except the Ritz crackers). Pour into an ungreased baking dish or pie plate. Bake for 30 minutes or until bubbly. Serve with Ritz crackers.

stuffed mushrooms
makes 2 dozen

Stuffed mushrooms make a hearty appetizer. When choosing mushrooms, select nice, fresh white ones approximately 1½-inches in diameter. Clean the mushrooms before using by gently wiping them with a damp paper towel.

24 white mushrooms
¼ cup ham, chopped
½ onion, finely diced
1 teaspoon sherry
2 tablespoons butter
3 tablespoons bread crumbs

marinated mushrooms

Another great way to serve mushrooms is to marinate them. Keep the mushrooms whole and add enough Newman's Own Olive Oil and Vinegar Dressing to just cover them. Serve either at room temperature or chilled. They're a great appetizer.

Remove the mushroom stems from the caps and set the caps aside. Finely chop the mushroom stems.

To prepare the filling, melt butter in a large skillet over medium heat. Add the chopped mushroom stems, ham, onion and sherry. Cook approximately 5 minuted until tender. Stir in the bread crumbs.

Stuff the mushroom caps with the filling.

When ready to serve, preheat the oven to 350°. Place mushrooms (stuffed side up) on a baking sheet. Bake for 15 minutes.

bill's famous bacon and horseradish dip
serves a crowd

This is such a typical bachelor dip. We've been to many parties given by bachelors where this kind of dip is served. It is the quintessential bachelor's appetizer!

8 slices bacon, cooked until crisp and crumbled
1 container (16 ounces) sour cream
1 tablespoon horseradish
dash of garlic powder
dash of onion salt
dash of cayenne
dash of paprika
ruffled potato chips or Fritos

Mix all the ingredients together and refrigerate until ready to serve. Serve with ruffled potato chips or Fritos. If you want to be really healthy, serve with crudité (raw sliced vegetables such as carrots, celery, green, red and yellow bell peppers, broccoli, cauliflower). Sprinkle with paprika.

---

onion dip

1 package onion soup mix (*I prefer Lipton's*)
1 container (16 ounces) of sour cream
8 slices bacon, cooked until crisp and crumbled

Mix all ingredients together. Chill until ready to serve. Serve with ruffled potato chips or Fritos.

---

mr. p's smoky pecans

serves

My friend Mike is a fabulous cook and hysterically funny. Last year I was the "talent" (I use this term loosely) for the cooking stage at a local home and garden show. Arriving Thursday evening for my first gig I realized I was the *only* "talent" for the weekend. I immediately called Mike and persuaded him to join me on stage. He graciously agreed and we had a million laughs.

This is a treat Mike prepares each Christmas and gives as gifts to his friends. Friends usually return the container to ensure they're on the gift list the following year! We're lucky enough to be on his holiday gift list and anxiously await the arrival of the pecans each year.

2 pounds raw pecan halves	1 tablespoon hot curry powder
6 tablespoons butter	½ tablespoon garlic powder
3 tablespoons Worcestershire sauce	1 tablespoon kosher salt
1 tablespoon chili powder	5 tablespoons liquid smoke

Preheat the oven to 325°.

Melt butter in a saucepan over medium heat. Remove from heat and stir in all ingredients except the nuts and 2 tablespoons of liquid smoke.

Add pecans and toss until coated. Spread out on a lightly greased cookie sheet.

Roast for 35 – 40 minutes. Toss every 10 minutes, brushing with remaining liquid smoke to enhance flavor.

Remove and let cool completely. Store in a Ziploc bag in refrigerator for up to one week. Pecans are a great snack for a holiday party, watching the ball game or a picnic.

spiced shrimp

serves 4

Half the fun of eating spiced shrimp is the warm conversation that comes with friends are sitting around a table covered with newspaper peeling and eating the shrimp then washing down with a cold beer or glass of wine.

1 pound raw shrimp, shells on
2 tablespoons Old Bay Seasoning
2 teaspoon cayenne pepper
cocktail sauce

cocktail sauce

½ cup ketchup
1 tablespoon horseradish
1 teaspoon lemon juice
Tabasco sauce to taste
Worcestershire sauce to taste

Mix all ingredients together. That's it.

Toss the shrimp with Old Bay and cayenne pepper.

Place a steamer in a medium saucepan. Fill with water to just below the base of the steamer. Bring the water to a boil then add the shrimp. Cover the saucepan with a tight fitting lid. Turn the heat to low and cook for 2 – 3 minutes or until the shrimp turn pink. Be careful not to overcook them, they will turn mushy.

To serve, toss on a table covered with newspaper. Let everyone dig in and get their fingers dirty.

Clean up is a cinch—toss the newspaper in the trash. Clean your hands easily by squeezing lemon juice in your palm, rubbing your hands together then rinsing with soapy water.

grills with
makes 1

The University Diner (The U.D.) was on the edge of the University of Virginia campus and frequently the last stop in the wee hours of the morning before stumbling back to your dorm or fraternity house. Anyone who either attended or frequented UVA will certainly remember it. Our friends Stacy and Carter (of Carter's Poor Man's Dinner page 92) recall with fond memories many late night U.D. stops with the waitress barking at them to hurry up and order.

The grills with was a popular item on the menu with contests held to see how many one could eat in one seating. Bill's personal best was seven; Carter's and my brother-in law Ted's was five. I don't know if the U.D. is still there, but if you find yourself in Charlottesville, VA, and it's still open, grab a grills with.

1 glazed donut (*I prefer Krispy Kreme, who doesn't?!*)
1 teaspoon butter
1 scoop vanilla ice cream

Melt butter in a skillet over medium heat. Place the donut in the pan. Let warm for 1 – 2 minutes. Flip. Let warm on the other side. Place on a plate and top with a scoop of vanilla ice cream.

drunken melon
serves 8

This is a great refreshing snack on a hot summer evening.

    1 cantaloupe melon, seeds removed, cut into 1-inch pieces
    1 honeydew melon, seeds removed, cut into 1-inch pieces
    1 small watermelon, cut into 1-inch pieces
    ¼ cup vodka

Toss the melon pieces together in a bowl with vodka. Refrigerate until ready to serve.

entrées

carter's poor man's dinner - 92

tom's ramen - 92

todd's meat loaf - 93

yankee pot roast - 94

corned beef and cabbage - 95

calf's liver smothered with onions - 96

rustic short ribs - 97

rosemary and thyme slow roasted prime rib - 99

baked chicken with onions - 100

breaded pork chops - 101

pork tenderloin with brandy sauce - 102

broiled salmon - 103

sole meunière - 104

shrimp scampi - 105

crab cakes - 106

broiled scallops with linguini - 107

most of you probably have a repertoire of pasta dishes. This chapter intentionally has only one. The goal of this chapter is to break you of the pasta habit and give you more variety.

While the fish chapter of my first book, *the tiny kitchen cooking and entertaining* reads, "Not in the tiny kitchen, it smells." This book has several fish recipes. I am allergic to shellfish and don't cook much fish inside (because sometimes it does smell). Fish is healthy, easy to prepare and a nice option when you want a lighter meal.

Bill urges you to try his favorite, shrimp scampi. The best he ever tasted was in Barcelona, Spain. The concierge at the hotel recommended a fabulous restaurant down a back alley. The proprietors didn't speak much English and we didn't speak *any* Spanish. We were seated in a back room by the kitchen; it was obvious this room was for foreigners. There was a Japanese family, a couple of German businessmen and us. The front room, which was empty, was for locals. We relied on the proprietor's recommendations for ordering (we didn't *read* Spanish either). We were sure he was thinking, "Stupid Americans. I will serve them the most expensive items on the menu!" He brought a bottle of wine that was the best wine we have ever had and we were sure it was at least $150. Bill had an appetizer portion of scampi, which was about a dozen jumbo shrimp, sizzling in a garlic sauce which was scrumptious. One course was better than the next and we were sure the bill was going to be $500; and it would have served us right, not knowing the language. When the bill arrived we were elated to find it was the equivalent of $75! The wine, it turns out, was only about $7. When we came home I immediately started testing scampi recipes with Bill as taster. He thinks the recipe here is pretty close to what he had in Barcelona.

For more entrées look in the Classics from the Original Tiny Kitchen chapter.

carter's poor man's dinner
serves 1

Our friend Carter ate this frequently when he was in college. When the funds are low, you have to make the most of every dollar. Carter preferred to spend his money on fun at the bars. So he'd eat this dinner before he went out. This concotion offered several advantages—not only was it quick and easy to make, inexpensive and only used one pot, but it had the added benefit of an all carbohydrate meal which absorbed the alcohol rather quickly.

1 cup Minute rice
1 cup water
1 can (11 ounces) corn, liquid drained
Worcestershire sauce to taste

Bring the water to a boil in a saucepan. Stir in the rice and cover. Remove the saucepan from the heat and let stand for 5 minutes. Stir in the corn and Worcestershire. Mix well.

tom's ramen
another poor man's dinner

Our friend Tom is an excellent cook and can make anything, but insisted a book for bachelor's needed a ramen recipe. He jazzes his up by adding fresh veggies.

1 package (3 ounces) ramen noodles, any flavor.
1 cup of your favorite fresh vegetables, cooked and diced

Prepare the ramen noodles according to the directions on the package. Add the vegetables and serve.

todd's meatloaf
serves 4

This recipe is compliments of Todd Healy, the fabulous artist who did the cover illustrations for both this book and *the tiny kitchen*. He swears this is the meal that won over his wife Lorraine. Try it and see what happens.

1 ½ pounds lean ground beef
8 ounces (½ roll) spicy sausage (*Todd prefers Jimmy Dean*)
2 garlic cloves, crushed
¼ cup sliced black olives
½ cup cheddar cheese, shredded
½ cup Swiss cheese, shredded
½ cup oatmeal
2 eggs
Tabasco to taste
salt and pepper to taste
ketchup

Preheat the oven to 350°.

Mix all ingredients together in a large bowl except the ketchup. Shape into a loaf and place in a roasting pan. Spread a thin layer of ketchup on the top. Bake for 50 minutes.

To serve, slice in ½-inch slices. Serve with mashed potatoes (page 20) and green beans (page 31).

yankee pot roast
serves 4

Whenever we would visit my grandmother for the summer she would have a pot roast dinner waiting for us after our six-hour drive. Her house smelled so good from the aroma of the pot roast *and* her homemade bread. It tasted *soooo* good. Make this when you want a good old-fashioned meal.

1 chuck roast (about 3 pounds)
salt and pepper to taste
2 tablespoons vegetable oil
2 stalks celery, diced
2 onions, peeled and diced

3 carrots, peeled and sliced
2 tablespoons vinegar
2 tablespoons beef broth
2 tablespoons tomato paste

Preheat the oven to 350°.

Season the roast with salt and pepper. Heat the oil in a Dutch oven over medium heat. Add the roast and cook until browned—approximately 5 minutes per side.

Add the celery, onions and carrots. Mix the vinegar, beef broth and tomato paste until smooth, then pour over the roast. Place the lid on the Dutch oven and place on the middle rack of the oven. Roast for 3 – 3 ½ hours or until tender when pierced with a fork. Remove from the oven. Slice in ¼-inch slices. Spoon the vegetables and pan juices over the sliced meat. Serve with mashed potatoes (page 20).

corned beef and cabbage

serves 6

This is the typical St. Patty's day meal (served with green beer, of course!); but it's great for any dinner as a change of pace. Leftovers are great for making a reuben sandwich or a corned beef on rye.

    1 corned beef brisket (4 – 5 pounds)
    6 white potatoes, peeled and quartered
    2 carrots, peeled and cut into 2-inch pieces
    1 green cabbage, quartered and core removed
    mustard

Rinse beef brisket under cold water.

Place the brisket in a stockpot and cover with water. Bring to a boil and take off the scum that rises to the top. Cover and simmer for 3 – 4 hours or until tender when pierced with a fork. Remove from pot and place on a platter.

Add the potatoes, carrots and cabbage to the pot and simmer for approximately 15 minutes or until the potatoes are fork tender.

To serve, cut the brisket in ½-inch slices and top with mustard. Serve with potatoes, carrots and cabbage.

calf's liver smothered with onions
serves 1

My father is the only person I know who actually likes liver and onions. Periodically he would get a hankering for it so my mother would fix it. My mother *never* made special meals. You either ate what the pot cooked or you didn't eat. But there is an exception to every rule and this was the exception. When Dad got liver and onions, we all got something else. My father now goes to The Palm to get his periodic liver and onion fix. I assume since it's on the menu at The Palm there are people other than my father who like it.

    6 ounces calf's liver
    1 onion halved, then thinly sliced
    2 tablespoons butter
    4 pieces bacon, cooked and crumbled

Heat the butter in a sauté pan over medium heat. Add the onions and cook about 5 minutes until tender. Add the liver. Cook for 5 minutes each side until browned.

   To serve, place the liver on a plate, top with onions and bacon. Serve with mashed potatoes (page 20) and steamed spinach (page 31).

rustic short ribs
serves 4

This is a great dish to make on a cold, snowy winter afternoon. The very slow cooking method coupled with the variety of root vegetables makes for a very flavorful, tender dish.

12 beef short ribs cut into 3-inch pieces
3 cups cabernet sauvignon
2 tablespoons vegetable oil
2 tablespoons flour
1 teaspoon salt
½ teaspoon pepper
2 carrots, peeled and cut into 1-inch pieces
2 leeks, cut into 1-inch pieces
2 parsnips, peeled and cut into 1-inch pieces
2 small white turnips, peeled and quartered

2 onions, peeled and quartered
6 cloves garlic, peeled
3 bay leaves
2 teaspoons thyme
1 teaspoon sage
8 sprigs fresh parsley
2 tablespoons tomato paste
1 tablespoon dry mustard
6 cups beef broth

Preheat the oven to 350°.

Heat the cabernet sauvignon in a small saucepan over medium-high heat. When it begins to boil reduce the heat to medium and let it simmer until it is reduced by half.

Mix the flour, salt and pepper in a small bowl. Dredge the short ribs in the flour mixture.

Heat the oil in a Dutch oven over medium heat. Add the short ribs and cook until browned—approximately 5 minutes per side, then transfer to a plate.

Add the vegetables, bay leaves, thyme, sage and parsley and cook for 5 minutes until browned. Remove the vegetables and stir in the tomato paste, mustard and reduced wine until blended. Stir in the beef broth. Add the short ribs and vegetables. Turn the heat to high and bring to a boil.

Place the lid on the Dutch oven and place on the middle rack of the oven. Roast for 2 ½ hours.

Remove from oven and transfer the meat and vegetables to a bowl. Cover with foil to keep warm.

To make the sauce, bring the liquid to a boil over high heat and continue to boil until it thickens and is reduced by half.

To serve, place three short ribs and a spoonful of vegetables on each plate or shallow bowl, then ladle each with sauce. Serve with rustic bread and a glass of cabernet sauvignon.

rosemary and thyme slow roasted prime rib

serves 6

The slow roasting method takes a long time but it is worth the wait. Slow roasting ensures even cooking throughout.

1 rib roast (5 pounds)
salt and pepper
1 garlic clove, peeled
2 tablespoons rosemary
2 tablespoons thyme
1 onion, peeled and quartered
2 carrots, peeled and cut into 1-inch pieces
2 cups beef broth

Preheat the oven to 250°.

Season the roast well by rubbing it all over with salt, pepper and garlic. Sprinkle the top with rosemary and thyme. Place in a roasting pan and add the onions, carrots, garlic and beef broth. Roast for 3 - 3½ hours or until the a meat thermometer reads 120° for rare, 125° to 130° for medium rare, 140° for medium and 150° for well done. Periodically check the roast and add beef broth when the pan becomes dry. Let cool 5 minutes before slicing. Serve with mashed potatoes (page 20) and green beans (page 31). Top with the pan drippings.

baked chicken with onions

serves 4

I made this recipe one day when I had a package of chicken that needed to be cooked before it spoiled. I had almost nothing in the refrigerator—except onions. I sliced them very thin, smothered them over the chicken, covered the chicken and baked it.

To my surprise the chicken was delightfully flavored. The slow cooking brought out the natural sugar in the onions which penetrated the chicken just enough to give it a nice flavor.

 4 boneless chicken breasts
 2 onions, halved and sliced very thin

Preheat the oven to 350°.

Place the chicken in a baking dish. Liberally spread the onion slices over the chicken so it is completely covered. Cover the baking dish tightly with aluminum foil. Bake for 30 – 35, depending on the size of the chicken breasts.

breaded pork chops
serves 4

This is one of Bill's signature dishes. He made this for me on our first Christmas Eve together. Occasionally he'll surprise me with this dish and have dinner waiting for me when I get home from work.

  4 lean pork chops (1-inch thick)
  1 egg
  3 tablespoons milk
  ¾ cup Italian style bread crumbs
  ¼ cup olive oil
  1 can (14.5 ounces) sauerkraut
  1 jar (24 ounces) applesauce

Preheat the oven to 350°.

  Beat the egg and milk together until thoroughly mixed. Dip the pork chops in the egg mixture then into the bread crumbs. Coat liberally.

  Heat the olive oil over medium-high heat in a large sauté pan. Place the pork chops in the pan and cook for 3 minutes per side or until the bread crumbs form a nice brown crust. Remove from the sauté pan and place on a broiler pan. Place in the oven and bake for 25 minutes. Serve with steamed broccoli (page 31), applesauce, sauerkraut and old-fashioned mashed potatoes (page 20).

pork tenderloin with brandy sauce

serves 4

Pork tenderloin is such an easy meal to fix. The brandy sauce is delicious. If you don't want to fuss with making it, use McCormick Green Peppercorn Sauce—it's very good. Served with steamed carrots and applesauce—it's a nice meal.

    2 boneless pork tenderloins (1 – 2 pounds each)
    brandy sauce

Preheat the oven to 350°.

    Place the tenderloin in a roasting pan. Roast for 40 minutes. Let cool for 5 minutes before slicing. Spoon the brandy sauce over the sliced pork.

brandy sauce

    2 shallots, diced
    2 teaspoons butter
    2 cups beef broth
    2 tablespoons frozen apple juice concentrate
    2 tablespoons brandy
    ½ cup of heavy cream, optional

Melt the butter in a small saucepan over medium heat. Sauté the shallots for 10 minutes until golden brown. Add the beef broth and apple juice concentrate. Bring to a boil over high heat and continue to boil until it is reduced by half. Add the brandy and cook for 5 minutes. For a thicker sauce, add the cream with the brandy and stir until it thickens. Do not let it boil.

broiled salmon
serves 4

This is another recipe from my friend Mike. It is so easy to make and is delicious (see the tempting photograph in the middle of the book). This recipe is great for a variety of fish such as flounder, swordfish, tuna, etc.

4 salmon fillets (6 ounces each)
½ cup mayonnaise
1 tablespoon chopped capers
1 tablespoon chopped fresh parsley
1 teaspoon lemon juice
¼ teaspoon cayenne pepper
¼ teaspoon salt

Preheat the broiler.

Combine all ingredients (except the salmon!) in a small bowl. Mix well.

Line a baking dish with aluminum foil (it makes for easy cleanup!). Lightly grease the aluminum foil with butter. Place the salmon in the baking dish and spread each with the mayonnaise mixture.

Broil for 10 – 12 minutes until the top is slightly brown and the fish is firm to the touch. Serve with steamed broccoli (page 31) and a glass of chilled chardonnay.

sole meunière
serves 4

4 fillets of sole (4 ounces each)
3 tablespoons flour
⅛ teaspoon salt
⅛ teaspoon pepper
2 tablespoons butter
2 tablespoons vegetable oil
1 tablespoon lemon juice
1 tablespoon capers
2 tablespoons chopped parsley

Mix the flour, salt and pepper. Coat each fillet with the flour mixture.

Melt the butter and oil over medium-high heat. When the butter begins to foam add the fish. Sauté for 1 – 2 minutes. Turn carefully and sauté for another 1 – 2 minutes. Remove the fish from the pan and sprinkle with parsley. Add the lemon juice and capers to the pan. Stir, then spoon over the fish. Serve with dilled new potatoes (page 21).

shrimp scampi
serves 2

This is one of Bill's favorite. It is derived from a restaurant in Barcelona, Spain.

    1 pound large shrimp, shelled (but keep the tails on) and deveined
    ¼ cup olive oil
    6 tablespoons butter
    4 cloves garlic, minced
    2 shallots, finely diced
    3 tablespoons chopped fresh parsley
    1 tablespoon crushed red pepper flakes
    2 tablespoons white wine
    2 tablespoons lemon juice

Melt the butter in a saucepan over medium heat. Add the olive oil, garlic, shallots, parsley, red pepper flakes, white wine and lemon juice and heat to a simmer.

Place the shrimp in a baking dish. Pour the butter sauce over the shrimp. Bake for 5 minutes. Turn the oven to broil and broil for 5 minutes.

crab cakes
serves 4

1 pound lump crab meat
1 cup bread crumbs
1 teaspoon dry mustard
⅛ teaspoon paprika
⅛ teaspoon cayenne pepper
2 teaspoons Old Bay seasoning
1 teaspoon lime juice
1 medium onion, finely diced
1 jalapeno pepper, diced
1 clove garlic, minced (optional)
3 tablespoons butter

tartar sauce

1 cup mayonnaise
1 whole dill pickle, finely chopped
2 teaspoons capers
1 tablespoon chives
1 teaspoon lemon juice

Combine all ingredients. Stir until well mixed. Keep refrigerated until ready to use.

Mix all ingredients *except* the crab meat and butter in a bowl. Blend well. Add the crab meat and gently mix just until blended. Don't over mix; the crab meat will fall apart and you want nice chunks.

Make 8 crab cakes about 2½ -inches in diameter and ½-inch thick.

Melt the butter in a large sauté pan over medium heat until it begins to sizzle. Add the crab cakes. Cook for 3 minutes until golden brown. Turn and cook another 3 minutes until well browned. Serve with tartar sauce.

broiled scallops with linguini

serves 4

20 sea scallops
3 tablespoons butter
2 cloves garlic, minced
½ cup white wine
2 cups linguini, cooked

Preheat the broiler.

Melt the butter in a sauté pan over medium heat. Add garlic and cook 2 – 3 minutes until tender. Add the scallops and sauté for 1 – 2 minutes per side. Transfer the scallops to a broiler pan and place under the broiler. Broil 30 seconds per side until browned. Scallops should be firm to the touch.

While the scallops are broiling add the wine to the sauté pan and heat through for 1 – 2 minutes.

Toss the scallops and wine sauce with the linguini. Serve with a Caesar salad and garlic bread.

garlic bread

1 loaf fresh crusty French or
   Italian bread
4 tablespoons butter
2 cloves garlic, minced

Preheat the oven to 350º.

Melt butter in a small saucepan over low heat. Add the garlic.

Cut the bread in 1-inch slices, cutting ⅞ of the way through. Brush the garlic butter in between the slices. Wrap the bread in foil and bake for 10 minutes.

grillin'

bratwurst - 112

grilled portobello sandwich - 113

barbecued ribs - 114

barbecued chicken - 115

jerk chicken - 115

grilled new york strips - 116

blackened pork tenderloin - 117

shish kebab - 118

lobster tails - 119

swordfish with tropical salsa - 120

tuna steaks with honey soy marinade - 121

potato and onion skewers - 122

grilled veggie medley - 123

grillin' is a guy thing. I've noticed it is very territorial; every guy I know has his own way to grill. No guy wants another guy touching his grill.

Whether you're using a tiny hibachi on the terrace, the el cheapo drug store collapsible, disposable grill, the traditional Weber kettle grill (in red, of course) or the fancy six-burner gas grill which duplicates a kitchen, the flavor of grilled food is unbeatable.

The challenge of true grillin' is to be able to grill several foods such as hot dogs, burgers and chicken, and have them all cooked to their desired doneness and served hot, *simultaneously*. This is part common sense, part skill and part luck. Common sense tells you to put food on first that takes the longest to cook. The trick is to prepare a grill for direct and indirect cooking (see page 110). Once the coals are ready and before you start cooking, keep one section of the grill with just a few coals, just enough to keep food warm. Put the chicken on to cook first. Once it's almost finished, move it to the warm side of the grill. It will continue to cook and stay hot without overcooking. Pile the pieces on top of each other to make room for the burgers and dogs. Once the burger and dogs are done, take all the food off the grill—hot!

Nothing tastes better than ribs cooked on the grill. They're always the first thing to go at a party; you never seem to have enough. Since they are somewhat fatty they can be difficult to cook over an open flame without burning. Not long after we were married I was grilling ribs for dinner. I put them on the heated grill, then went in the kitchen to putter. I looked out the window and noticed flames coming out of the grill. By the time I got there the ribs were completely charred. I thought it was hysterical—there went dinner! What can I say? I'm not a guy; grillin' isn't second nature to me.

Foods you can grill, marinades, seasonings and rubs are endless. What I have presented here is a variety of meat, poultry, fish, shellfish and vegetables to get you started. Most foods taste great with just the grilled flavor and no seasonings. Experiment with different food, seasoning and rub combinations.

The Williams-Sonoma Complete Grilling Cookbook best describes how to set up a fire for direct and indirect-heat cooking and for fire safety:

direct versus indirect heat

Before you begin grilling, determine if you will need direct or indirect heat. For either method, once the fire bed is ready, set the metal rack or grid on which the food will cook 4 - 6 inches above the heat.

Foods cooked with direct heat are placed directly over the hot coals or burners of the grill. Use this method for searing and for grilling small or thin food items that take less than 25 minutes to cook, including some poultry pieces, steaks, chops, burgers, sausages, fish fillets, and kabobs.

To set up a direct-heat fire in a charcoal grill, use long-handled metal tongs, a long poker, or another safe tool to spread hot coals evenly across the area of the fire pan directly below where the food will sit. For a direct-heat fire in a gas grill, heat the burners beneath the rack on which you plan to cook.

Indirect heat cooks foods by reflected heat, much like a roasting oven. Use this method for grilling larger pieces of foods such as a boneless leg of lamb or a whole chicken. Heat circulating inside the grill cooks the food more slowly and evenly, although you may turn the food part way through the cooking time to ensure uniform cooking and to distribute appetizing grill marks.

To set up an indirect-heat fire in a charcoal grill, place a drip pan (an aluminum-foil roasting pan is ideal) on the fire grate and use long-handled tongs to position the hot coals around the edge of the pan. Then put the food directly on the grill rack over the pan and cover the grill. For foods that require more than 40 minutes or more of cooking time, light a second batch of coals in another grill or other fireproof container and use them to replenish the fire as the first batch of coals dies out.

For an indirect-heat fire in a gas grill, first heat the grill using all the burners, then turn off any burners directly beneath where the food will cook and put a drip pan on the fire grate. Replace the grill rack, put the food over the drip pan, and adjust the burners on either side of the food to equal amounts of heat.

fire safety

Whenever you grill, keep the following in mind:

- From the moment you ignite the coals to the moment you dispose of the cooled ashes, never leave your grill unwatched or unattended.

- Always keep children and pets safely away from the grill.

- Do not wear loose clothing when grilling, and if you have long hair, tie it back.

- Always use your grill out in the open on a level surface, well clear of enclosures, overhangs, or anything combustible.

- Use only fire starters specifically designed for grill use. Other fuels, such as kerosene or gasoline, should not be placed anywhere near an outdoor grill.

- Do not use chimney or electric-coil starters with instant-lighting briquettes.

- If using an electric-coil starter, as soon as the coals are lit, unplug it and place it on a fireproof surface, well clear of anything flammable or of anyone who might accidentally touch it, until completely cool. Follow the same precautions for a chimney starter.

bratwurst

A grilled bratwurst doused with sauerkraut, chopped onions and lots of mustard washed down with an ice cold beer tastes great on a chilly fall afternoon.

Boiling the bratwursts in beer before grilling gives them a nice flavor and partially cooks them, making the grilling time shorter.

6 bratwursts
1 bottle beer (*not light*)
1 can (14.5 ounces) sauerkraut
1 onion, chopped
mustard
6 hot dog buns

Prepare the grill for direct-heat cooking.

Pour the beer into a medium saucepan, add the bratwursts and bring to a boil over high heat. Boil for 5 minutes.

Remove bratwursts from pan, place on grill and grill for 10 minutes, turning frequently to avoid burning and to ensure even browning.

Serve on hot dog buns and top with sauerkraut, chopped onion and mustard.

---

alternative serving suggestion

Grilled bratwurst is a great appetizer. Slice grilled bratwursts into bite size pieces. Serve with a side of mustard.

---

grilled portobello mushroom sandwich
serves 2

This is a great alternative to a hamburger. It's flavorful, hearty and for those watching their beer gut, has fewer calories.

2 portobello mushrooms
1 red onion, cut into 2-inch slices
balsamic vinegar
6 ounces goat cheese
2 hamburger buns

Prepare the grill for direct-heat cooking.

Brush the mushrooms on both sides with balsamic vinegar. Grill the mushrooms and red onion slices for 5 minutes per side until tender.

To serve, place the mushroom on the hamburger bun, top with grilled mushroom, red onion and goat cheese.

barbecued ribs
serves 4

Precooking ribs slowly in a very low oven allows much of the fat to drain and the meat to cook thoroughly. The grill provides the finishing touches, crisping up the ribs and adding that mouth watering charcoal flavor.

There are so many great barbecue sauces available today there is no need to make your own. Try a few and pick your own favorite.

   3 pounds pork spare ribs
   1 teaspoon chili powder
   1 teaspoon paprika
   1 teaspoon garlic powder
   1 teaspoon onion powder
   barbecue sauce (*I prefer Kraft Original*)

Preheat the oven to 250°.

To make the rub, mix chili powder, paprika, garlic powder and onion powder together.

Season the ribs liberally with the rub. Place the ribs in a roasting pan and bake for 2 hours. This can be done the day before and refrigerated until ready to eat.

Prepare the grill for direct-heat cooking.

To finish off the ribs, spread them liberally with barbecue sauce. Place on a hot grill and cook about 10 minutes per side until crispy.

barbecued chicken
serves 4

Barbecued chicken is a summertime favorite. What would a Fourth of July cook-out be without barbecued chicken? I've gotten in the habit of using boneless chicken breasts, but I do love chicken legs and thighs barbecued as well.

  4 boneless chicken breasts
  barbecue sauce (*I prefer Kraft Original*)

Prepare the grill for indirect-heat cooking.
  Place the chicken on the grill. Baste with barbecue sauce. Grill for 20 – 25 minutes, turning and basting with barbecue sauce frequently.
  The chicken is done when clear juices run when pricked. Serve with Bill's cole slaw (page 18).

> ## jerk chicken
>
> For grilled chicken with a kick, substitute either a dry jerk rub or a wet jerk seasoning for the barbecue sauce. Both types of jerk seasoning are available in the spice aisle of your grocer.

grilled new york strips
serves 2

Every once in a while I get a hankering for a big, thick juicy steak on the grill. Nothing else will do.

2 New York strip steaks (10 ounces and 1½-inches thick each)
onion powder
garlic powder
kosher salt

Prepare the grill for direct-heat cooking.

Generously season the steaks on both sides with onion powder, garlic powder and salt.

Place the steaks on the grill. Grill for 5 minutes per side for rare. Increase cooking time to 7 minutes per side for medium and 9 minutes per side for well done.

blackened pork tenderloin
serves 6

Pork tenderloin is a great alternative to beef or chicken. The tenderloin is tender, juicy and low in fat. It is particularly good on the grill.

1 boneless pork tenderloin
2 tablespoons cajun seasoning or blackening seasoning

Prepare the grill for indirect-heat cooking.

Generously season the tenderloin with cajun or blackening seasoning.

Place the tenderloin on the grill. Grill for 20 – 25 minutes turning frequently to ensure even cooking and to prevent it from burning. Let stand for 5 minutes before slicing.

To serve, slice in ¼ inch slices. Serve with Brooklyn potato salad (page 19) and a tossed salad.

shish kebab
serves 6

Metal skewers are preferable for cooking shish kebab on the grill. Bamboo skewers can be used but are not as sturdy. If you do use the bamboo skewers soak them in cold water for 30 minutes which will prevent them from burning and breaking.

I call for lamb in this recipe but beef or chicken can easily be substituted.

Boneless leg of lamb (2 pounds) cut into 1½-inch cubes
1 red onion, cut into chunks
1 pint cherry tomatoes
18 white mushrooms
1 *each* green and red peppers cut into 1½ x 1½-inch pieces, seeds removed
1 cup Newman's Own Olive Oil and Vinegar Dressing
3 cups cooked white rice (page 23)

Marinate the lamb in Newman's Own Olive Oil and Vinegar Dressing in a Ziploc bag in the refrigerator for at least one hour.

Prepare the grill for direct-heat cooking.

To assemble kebabs, alternate lamb, onions, cherry tomatoes, mushrooms and peppers until the skewers are filled to within an inch from the end.

Grill the kebabs for 25 – 30 minutes, turning frequently to cook evenly.

To serve, slide the lamb and vegetables off the skewers onto a bed of rice on individual serving plates.

lobster tails
serves 4

Lobster anytime is a real treat. Lobster on the grill is especially tempting. Although an old fashioned lobster bake is a lot of fun to prepare and to eat, lobster tails on the grill are much less messy all the way around. Besides, it's the best part of the lobster.

    4 lobster tails (10 ounces each)
    ½ cup butter
    1 tablespoon lemon juice
    1 shallot, finely diced

Prepare the grill for indirect-heat grilling.

In a small saucepan melt the butter over low heat. Stir in the lemon juice and shallots.

Using scissors cut each lobster tail lengthwise to expose the lobster meat. Drizzle the butter mixture over the meat, reserving half for serving with the cooked lobster.

Place the lobster tails on the grill and cover the grill. Cook for 10 minutes until the shells turn red and the meat is white all the way through.

To serve, place a lobster tail on each plate and drizzle with the remaining butter sauce. Serve with potato and onion skewers (page 122) and grilled corn (page 123).

swordfish with tropical salsa
serves 4

4 swordfish steaks (6 – 8 ounces and 1-inch thick each)
1 mango, finely diced
½ cup finely diced pineapple
1 jalapeno pepper, finely diced
1 teaspoon lime juice
2 tablespoons chopped fresh cilantro

Prepare the grill for direct-heat cooking.

Combine the mango, pineapple, jalapeno, lime juice and cilantro. Mix well. Refrigerate until ready to use.

Place the swordfish steaks on the grill. Grill for 5 minutes. Turn and grill for an additional 5 minutes. Remove from the grill.

Serve swordfish steaks topped with a spoonful of tropical salsa and accompany with assorted veggies on the grill (page 123).

tuna steaks with honey soy marinade
serves 4

4 tuna steaks (6 – 8 ounces and 1-inch each
½ cup honey
½ cup soy sauce (*I prefer lite, it's not quite as salty*)
1 garlic clove, minced
1 teaspoon lime juice

Prepare the grill for direct-heat cooking.

Combine the honey, soy sauce, garlic and lime juice. Mix well. Marinate the tuna steaks for 15 minutes.

Place the tuna steaks on the grill. Grill for 5 minutes. Turn and grill for an additional 5 minutes. Remove from the grill.

Serve with grilled corn on the cob (page 123).

potato and onion skewers
serves 4

This makes a nice side dish for any grilled meat, poultry or fish.

16 small, new red potatoes, approximately 1½-inches in diameter
2 red onions, cut into quarters, then halved
¼ cup olive oil
3 tablespoons chopped fresh rosemary
salt and pepper to taste

Wash the potatoes and boil for 15 minutes in salted water until fork tender. Pour out the water and let cool.

Mix the olive oil, rosemary and salt and pepper together.

Prepare the grill for direct-heat cooking.

To assemble the skewers (if using bamboo skewers see page 118 for preparation) alternate potatoes and onions.

Place the assembled skewers on the prepared grill and brush with olive oil mixture.

Grill for 15 – 20 minutes, turning frequently to cook and brown evenly.

grilled veggie medley
serves 4

You can grill any variety of fresh vegetables. Be sure to cut them in slices or chunks large enough so they won't slip through the slats of the grill.

    1 red or yellow bell pepper, cut lengthwise in 1-inch pieces, seeds removed
    1 red onion or sweet vidalia onion
    1 eggplant, cut into 2 -inch slices
    1 summer squash
    8 stalks asparagus
    8 white mushrooms
    2 ears corn, each cut into quarters
    2 tomatoes, cut in half
    1 cup Newman's Own Olive Oil and Vinegar Dressing

Prepare a grill for direct-heat grilling.
    Marinate the vegetables in Newman's Own Olive Oil and Vinegar Dressing for 15 minutes. Place vegetables directly on the grill. Grill for 5 – 7 minutes turning frequently.

---

grilled corn on the cob

Remove the husks from the corn. Place in salted boiling water and boil for 8 minutes. Finish off on the grill, grilling for 10 minutes, turning frequently.

---

dessert

ice

cream.

any

flavor.

cocktails

7 & 7 - 130	gibson - 131	mojito - 133
amaretto sour - 130	gimlet - 131	old-fashioned - 134
bacardi cocktail - 130	gin & tonic - 132	piña colada - 134
belfast bailey's - 130	harvey wallbanger - 132	planters punch - 134
bellini - 130	hot buttered rum - 132	rob roy - 134
black russian - 130	hot toddy - 132	sangria - 134
bloody bull - 130	hurricane - 132	scotch & soda - 134
bloody mary - 130	irish coffee - 132	screwdriver - 134
boilermaker - 131	kir - 132	sea breeze - 135
cape codder - 131	long island iced tea - 133	shirley temple - 135
cc & ginger - 131	madras - 133	silver bullet - 135
champagne cocktail - 131	mai tai - 133	sombrero - 135
cosmopolitan - 131	manhattan - 133	tom collins - 135
cuba libra - 131	martini - 133	white russian - 135
daiquiri - 131	mimosa - 133	wine cooler - 135
egg nog - 131	mint julep - 133	zombie - 135

there isn't a guy I know who doesn't love his cocktail. My father's before dinner drink is an Old Grandad Manhattan on the rocks. After dinner it's scotch on the rocks with a splash of soda. Bill likes his Friday night martini and the ceremony that goes along with it. He starts by filling two martini glasses with ice and water to chill the glasses. Then he fills a cocktail shaker with ice and pours in a liberal serving of gin (Beefeaters or Bombay Saffire) and shakes seven times. He empties the ice water from one of the glasses, strains the martini into the chilled glass, spritzes the top with dry vermouth and garnishes with jalapeno stuffed olives. The shaker goes into the freezer until he's ready for round two for the second chilled glass.

Like Alan Jackson sings, "It's five o'clock somewhere."

shaken or stirred? straight-up or on the rocks?...

...Ginger or Mary Ann? The answer is the same for all of these questions. Neither is better than the other, it's just a matter of personal taste and preference and what you're in the mood for.

prepping and hints

Many times a glass needs to be prepped before serving a cocktail, such as prechilling a glass for a martini. Here are a few prepping hints.

pre-chilling a glass. To pre-chill a glass, fill it with ice cubes and water for 3 minutes. Pour out the ice water just prior to pouring the cocktail.

rimming the glass with salt or sugar. To rim a glass with salt or sugar, rub a piece of lemon around the rim of the glass. Then dip the rim in either salt or sugar.

sugar water. To prepare sugar water add 1 cup of sugar to 4 cups of water. Heat in a saucepan over medium heat until the sugar dissolves.

You could fill your bar with nearly twenty types of glasses, including red wine, white wine, cordial, highball, collins, old-fashioned, double old-fashioned, margarita, cocktail, brandy snifter, and the list goes on. The chances are, with a tiny kitchen you do not have room for such a variety of glasses. If you're a frequent entertainer, the well stocked tiny bar should consist of:

liquors

beer
bourbon
brandy
gin
Irish whiskey
rum, dark and light
scotch
sherry
tequila
triple sec
vermouth, dry and sweet
vodka
whiskey
wine, red and white

garnishes & condiments

cocktail olives
cocktail onions
grenadine
lemons
limes
maraschino cherries
margarita salt
oranges
sugar
Tabasco sauce
Worcestershire sauce

mixers

assorted soda
bitters
club soda
collins mix
cranberry juice
grapefruit juice
lemon juice
lime juice
orange juice
tonic water

barware

bar strainer
bottle opener
champagne flutes or saucers
cocktail (martini) glasses
cocktail shaker
corkscrew
highball glasses
ice bucket & tongs
jigger
old-fashioned glasses
shot glasses
wine glasses

This chapter could be a book in itself. What is presented here is a wide variety of common cocktails. There are many adaptations for these drinks, particularly the martinis. You should be able to accommodate any guest with this list.

For a complete bartending resource visit www.webtender.com.

7 & 7

2 ounces Seagrams 7
2 ounces 7-Up

Combine Seagrams 7 and
7-Up over ice in an old-
fashioned glass. Stir.

amaretto sour

2 ounces amaretto
1 ounce lemon juice
orange slice

Combine amaretto and
lemon juice in a cocktail
shaker filled with ice.
Shake well. Strain into a
chilled cocktail glass.
Garnish with orange slice.

bacardi cocktail

2 ounces light Bacardi rum
1 teaspoon lemon juice
2 dashes grenadine

Combine all ingredients in a
cocktail shaker filled with
ice. Shake well. Strain into
a chilled cocktail glass.

belfast bailey's

Our friend Nancy's friends

Pauly and Hendi from
Belfast made this for us
while here on a visit.

5 ounces Irish whiskey
10 ounces water
1 can (14 ounces) con-
densed milk
2 tablespoons coffee

Combine all ingredients in a
jar or bottle with a lid.
Shake vigorously to blend.
Refrigerate. Keeps for up
to one month.
To serve, pour over ice in an
old-fashioned.

bellini

2 ounces chilled cham-
pagne
2 ounces peach nectar
1 teaspoon lemon juice

Pour peach nectar and
lemon juice into a chilled
champagne flute. Stir. Fill
the glass with champagne.
Stir gently.

black russian

2 ounces vodka
1 ounce coffee liqueur

Combine vodka and coffee
liqueur over ice in a double
old-fashioned glass. Stir.

bloody bull

2 ounces vodka
4 ounces tomato juice
4 ounces chilled beef broth
1 teaspoon lime juice
Tabasco, to taste
black pepper, to taste
lime wedge

Combine all ingredients
except lime wedge over ice
in a highball. Stir. Garnish
with lime wedge.

bloody mary

2 ounces vodka
6 ounces tomato juice
½ teaspoon lemon juice
½ teaspoon horseradish
black pepper, to taste
lime wedge
celery stalk

Combine all ingredients
except lime wedge and
celery over ice in a highball.
Stir. Garnish with lime
wedge and celery.

boilermaker

1 can (12 ounces) beer
1 shot whiskey

Pour beer into a frosty mug.
Pour whiskey into a shot
glass. Drop shot glass into
beer mug.

cape codder

2 ounces vodka
6 ounces cranberry juice
lime wedge

Combine vodka and cran-
berry juice over ice in a
highball. Stir. Garnish with
lime wedge.

cc & ginger (highball)

2 ounces Canadian Club
6 ounces ginger ale

Combine Canadian Club
and ginger ale over ice in a
double old-fashioned glass.
Stir.

champagne cocktail

½ teaspoon sugar
several dashes bitters
chilled champagne
lemon twist

Combine sugar and bitters
in a champagne flute. Fill
with chilled champagne.
Stir gently. Garnish with
lemon twist.

cosmopolitan

2 ounces vodka
1 ounce triple sec
1 ounce cranberry juice
dash of lime juice

Combine all ingredients in
cocktail shaker filled with
ice. Shake well. Strain into
a chilled cocktail glass.

cuba libre

2 ounces dark rum
4 ounces cola

Combine rum and cola over
ice in a double old-fash-
ioned glass. Stir.

daiquiri

2 ounces light rum
1 teaspoon lime juice
1 teaspoon sugar water
Combine all ingredients in a
cocktail shaker filled with
ice. Shake well. Strain into
a chilled cocktail glass.

egg nog

4 ounces egg nog (store
bought)
2 ounces brandy
1 scoop vanilla ice cream

Combine eggnog and
brandy into an old-fash-
ioned glass. Stir. Add ice
cream and sprinkle with
nutmeg.

gibson

3 ounces gin
dashes of dry vermouth, to
taste
3 cocktail onions

Combine gin and vermouth
in a cocktail shaker filled
with ice. Shake. Strain into
a chilled cocktail glass.
Garnish with cocktail
onions.

gimlet

3 ounces gin
1 ounce Roses lime juice

Combine gin and lime juice in a cocktail shaker filled with ice. Shake well. Strain into a chilled cocktail glass.

gin & tonic

2 ounces gin
2 ounces tonic water
lime wedge

Combine gin and tonic over ice in an old-fashioned glass. Stir. Garnish with lime.

harvey wallbanger

2 ounces vodka
4 ounces orange juice
1 ounce Galliano

Combine vodka and orange juice over ice in a highball. Stir. Top off with Galliano.

hot buttered rum

2 ounces dark rum
1 teaspoon brown sugar
1 teaspoon butter
boiling water
nutmeg

Place sugar in the bottom of a mug. Fill mug two-thirds with boiling water. Add rum. Stir. Top with butter and sprinkle with nutmeg.

hot toddy

3 ounces whiskey
1 tablespoon honey
1 tablespoon lemon juice
4 whole cloves
ground cinnamon, to taste
boiling water
nutmeg
cinnamon stick
lemon slice

Combine whiskey, honey, lemon juice, cloves and ground cinnamon in a mug. Mix together. Fill mug with boiling water. Stir. Sprinkle with nutmeg and garnish with cinnamon stick and lemon slice.

hurricane

4 ounces dark rum
4 ounces passion fruit syrup
1 tablespoon lime juice
dash of grenadine
orange slice
maraschino cherry

Combine rum, passion fruit syrup, lime juice and grenadine in a hurricane glass. Stir. Fill glass with crushed ice. Garnish with orange slice and maraschino cherry.

irish coffee

2 ounces Irish whiskey
black coffee
whipped cream
crème de cacao
sugar
lemon juice

Rim a mug with sugar. Pour in the Irish whiskey. Fill the mug with coffee. Top with whipped cream and crème de cacao.

kir

2 ounces crème de casis
white wine
lemon twist

Pour crème de casis over ice in a wine glass. Fill with wine. Garnish with lemon twist.

long island iced tea

2 ounces vodka
1 ounce gin
1 ounce tequila
1 ounce light rum
orange slice
½ ounce crème de menthe
2 ounces lemon juice
1 teaspoon sugar
cola
lime wedge

Combine all ingredients except cola and lime wedge in a cocktail shaker filled with ice. Shake well. Strain into a highball filled with ice. Fill with cola. Garnish with lime wedge.

madras

2 ounce vodka
3 ounces cranberry juice
3 ounces orange juice

Combine all ingredients over ice in a highball. Stir.

mai tai

2 ounces light rum
2 ounces dark rum
1 ounce Curacao
1 teaspoon grenadine

almond syrup
pineapple spear
paper umbrella (optional)

Combine all ingredients except pineapple wedge and paper umbrella in a cocktail shaker filled with ice. Shake well. Strain into a highball over ice. Garnish with pineapple spear and paper umbrella.

manhattan

2 ounces bourbon
½ ounce sweet vermouth
maraschino cherry

Combine bourbon and vermouth in a cocktail shaker filled with ice. Shake well. Strain into a chilled cocktail glass. Serve with a cherry.

martini

2 ounces dry gin
½ ounce dry vermouth
3 olives

Combine gin and vermouth in a cocktail shaker filled with ice. Shake well. Strain into a chilled cocktail glass. Garnish with olives.

mimosa

2 ounces chilled champagne
2 ounces fresh orange juice

Fill a champagne flute halfway with orange juice. Top off with champagne.

mint julep

3 ounces bourbon
1 tablespoon sugar water
6 fresh mint leaves, crushed
1 fresh mint sprig

Mix crushed mint leaves with sugar water in a highball. Fill with ice. Add bourbon. Stir well. Garnish with mint sprig.

mojito

2 ounces light rum
1 ounce lime juice
5 fresh mint leaves
dash of bitters

Combine all ingredients in a cocktail shaker filled with ice. Shake well. Strain into an old fashioned filled with ice.

old-fashioned

2 ounces bourbon
½ teaspoon sugar
1 teaspoon water
dash of bitters
lemon twist

Combine sugar, water, bitters in an old fashioned glass. Stir until sugar is dissolved. Add bourbon. Stir. Add ice cubes. Garnish with lemon twist.

piña colada

2 ounces light rum
1 ounce dark rum
3 ounces pineapple juice
2 ounces coconut cream
pineapple spear

Combine all ingredients except pineapple spear in a blender filled with ice. Blend until smooth. Pour into a highball. Garnish with pineapple spear.

planters punch

2 ounces light rum
2 ounces dark rum
1 ounce lemon juice
1 ounce lime juice

¼ teaspoon triple sec
dash of grenadine
1 teaspoon sugar
club soda
orange slice
lime slice
maraschino cherry
pineapple spear

Combine rums, lemon juice, lime juice, triple sec, grenadine and sugar in a cocktail shaker filled with ice. Shake well. Pour over ice into a highball. Fill with club soda. Stir. Garnish with orange slice, lime slice, cherry and pineapple spear.

rob roy

2 ounces scotch
1 ounce sweet vermouth
dash of bitters
maraschino cherry

Combine scotch, vermouth and bitters in a cocktail shaker filled with ice. Shake well. Strain into a chilled cocktail glass. Garnish with maraschino cherry.

sangria

2 bottles dry red wine (750 ml each)
4 ounces triple sec
3 ounces brandy
3 ounces orange juice
2 ounces lemon juice
4 ounces sugar water
1 quart club soda
2 limes, sliced
2 lemons, sliced
2 oranges, sliced

Combine all ingredients except fruit slices together in a pitcher. Chill. When ready to serve add club soda and ice cubes and garnish with fruit slices.

scotch & soda

2 ounces scotch
splash of club soda

Combine scotch and soda over ice in an old fashioned glass. Stir.

screwdriver

2 ounces vodka
4 ounces orange juice
orange slice
maraschino cherry

Combine vodka and orange

juice over ice in a highball. Stir. Garnish with orange slice and maraschino cherry.

sea breeze

2 ounces vodka
3 ounces cranberry juice
1 ounce grapefruit juice
orange slice
maraschino cherry

Combine vodka, cranberry juice and grapefruit juice over ice in a highball. Stir. Garnish with orange slice and maraschino cherry.

shirley temple

6 ounces ginger ale
1 teaspoon grenadine
1 orange slice
6 maraschino cherries
(yes, 6 cherries)
rock candy on a stick

Combine ginger ale and grenadine in a highball filled with ice. Stir. Garnish with orange slice, maraschino cherries, and rock candy.

silver bullet

2 ounces gin
1 ounce Jagermeister
1 teaspoon lemon juice

Combine all ingredients in a shaker filled with ice. Shake well. Strain into a chilled cocktail glass.

sombrero

2 ounces coffee liqueur
4 ounces half-and-half

Pour coffee liqueur over ice in an old-fashioned glass. Top off with half-and-half.

tom collins

2 ounces gin
4 ounces Collins mix
orange slice
maraschino cherry

Combine gin and Collins mix in a highball filled with ice. Stir. Garnish with orange slice and mara-schino cherry.

white russian

2 ounces vodka
2 ounces coffee liqueur
1 ounce half-and-half

Combine all in shaker filled with ice. Shake well. Strain into a chilled old-fashioned glass.

wine cooler

4 ounces white wine
2 ounces lemon lime soda

Combine wine and soda over ice in a wine glass. Stir.

zombie

2 ounces light rum
2 ounces dark rum
1 ounce 151-proof rum
1 ounce triple sec
1 teaspoon Pernod
1 ounce lime juice
1 ounce orange juice
1 ounce pineapple juice
1 ounce guava nectar
1 tablespoon grenadine
1 tablespoon almond syrup
fresh mint sprig
pineapple spear

Combine all ingredients in a cocktail shaker filled with ice. Shake well. Strain over ice into a highball. Garnish with mint sprig and pineapple spear.

the bachelor entertains

ntertaining! Bill and I, individually and as a couple, have always loved entertaining. We love gathering together with family and friends to celebrate holidays, special occasions or just for fun. Entertaining can be as simple and as small
as one or two friends or family for a few drinks before going on to another party
or out to a restaurant to larger, more formal occasions bringing together old and
new friends. It should never be viewed as a chore or reason to panic but rather as
much fun preparing as the event itself.

Just because you're a bachelor doesn't mean it's always okay to serve beer and
nuts out of the cans and pizza out of the box and call it entertaining or just plain
not do any at all. You have probably been entertained by married friends and
perhaps friends of your parents who invite you for a great dinner or to meet their
daughter. You want to reciprocate or may even feel that since you are a bachelor
you really don't have to—well, you do! You can always take them out to a restaurant but it's much more fun to have them to your place. You and probably most of
your friends are adults and as such should do things in a "grownup" way.

Here are some hints for making entertaining easier.

keep an orderly dwelling

Always keep your apartment or house orderly so that you will not be embarrassed
to invite people over on the spur of the moment or if someone just pops in. Get
rid of the newspapers and empty your trash cans every day. Keep books and
magazines neatly stacked on tables, under tables, next to chairs, under chairs, or if
you are lucky, in the bookcases; don't have them in the bathroom.

Keep dirty glasses, dishes and ash trys out of the living room and bedroom—
take them into the kitchen, and wash them, as you use them. Keep the bathroom
clean and have a supply of fresh hand towels available in a closet or drawer just for
guests. If you have only one bathroom keep your toilet articles together in a bas-

ket, or lucite box so that they can be quickly stashed in a closet or drawer when you have guests—they don't want to see those things on the counter! You will be ready for unexpected visitors and have a leg up on getting ready for scheduled entertaining.

you don't need all the right "things"

So you might not have all the "things" married friends may have. Don't let that deter you from entertaining. Keep things simple but tasteful. See the recommendations on pages 6,7,8, 11 and 128 for items to have on hand that will make entertaining easy. Plenty of friends, good food, drinks, music, conversation and a clean, pleasant environment make the event.

invitations

Issue an invitation that is appropriate for your event. For example if you're inviting people over for a casual, spur of the moment evening, a simple phone call or email will do. If you are planning a more elaborate "do" send a nice invitation at least two weeks in advance. Either buy attractive ones at a starionary store or create your own on the computer. Include pertinent information such as the purpose, date, time and location. Make sure you include an Rsvp and phone number on the invitation so you will have an accurate headcount of who is coming.

create an inviting atmosphere

Simple flowers or plants enhance the entertaining atmosphere. No, they're not too feminine. You can always pick up a couple of dozen fresh tulips, mums, lilies or whatever else is in season from the local supermarket or flower mart. Buy only one kind of flower and put them all in one plain glass vase or pitcher on the coffee table or in several plain glasses on small tables and one on the sink in the bathroom——use your imagination. Candles and appropriate music add to the atmosphere.

key items

Get an inexpensive collapsible table and keep it under your bed. An old-fashioned card table or a plastic patio round table are both very inexpensive and easy to store under the bed. Use it as a prep table, or extra counter space during preparation. I'd set mine up in the living room (no room in the kitchen) while I prepped and watched TV. As party time approached I'd set it up with an inexpensive cloth and it served as a bar or serving table.

Dishes and serving pieces don't have to be expensive and they don't need to match either. Clear glass dinner plates can be found for $1.00 apiece. Similarly, attractive platters, serving dishes and utensils can be found at bargain prices. These can all be stored in a box under the bed.

Take a look around at what you have and make the most out of it; improvise. A water pitcher suddenly becomes a vase for flowers; the TV is draped with a cloth and then poised with an attractive tray of appetizers.

My friend Alex who had a small apartment in Greenwich used to have an annual holiday cocktail party. To make more room for guests, he'd move all the living room furniture into the bedroom and take the door off the apartment. Be inventive and you'll be amazed at what you can do.

Have a great time entertaining!

setting the table

A table set correctly speaks volumes. In case you didn't have table setting duties as a kid growing up (we all did from the first grade!) the following diagram will guide you through. Make sure to set the table correctly the first time you make dinner for that someone special. You will earn major points!

a. salad plate
b. place mat
c. salad fork
d. dinner fork
e. napkin
f. dinner plate
g. dinner knife
h. spoon
i. water goblet
j. wine glass
k. butter spreader
l. butter plate

be a gracious host

Be a gracious host and make your guests feel welcome. Make sure you are ready at least fifteen minutes before they arrive. Once the guests arrive, be sure to take their coats and offer them a drink. Always have some non-alcoholic drinks available for non-drinkers and the designated drivers. Make sure you have enough ice!

If you have guests who don't know anyone, introduce them around and make sure they get engaged into conversation. If a guest has had too much to drink and should not be driving, take their keys and give them a place to sleep.

great entertainers

One of the things that attracted me to Bill was his love of entertaining. I invited him to a fajita and margarita party I was having; I had only met him a week or so before the party and I liked him. I thought this would be a good opportunity to see if we were compatible and if my friends and family liked him. He came over early the day of the party to help me prepare. He brought loads of firewood and some Mexican decorations to add to the party theme. He prepped food all day and when the party began he kept a fire roaring in the fireplace, the blenders going with the margaritas and cooked all the fajitas. The day after the party, he even came back and helped me clean up. I was smitten! *This* was the man for me. I found out he *loved* to entertain and did so frequently. In fact, to this day we still hold his Annual Strawberry Daiquiri Party (the first Saturday in June) which he started 26 years ago while he was in college.

Our friend, Mark, whom I have known since I was a kid (our dads were friends from West Point), was a bachelor for a long time before he finally met and married the love of his life, Kathy. After graduating from law school Mark took a job on The Hill and bought an apartment just across the Potomac in Arlington—it was in a high rise and had two balconies overlooking the city. It was very nicely furnished and had a fabulous view of Washington. He started having "Watch the Fireworks" parties on July 4th. We were all included—three generations—our parents, ours and the next generation of little children. It was always such fun. He'd set up a bar and terrific buffet with the food all very attractively arranged on the dining room table. Mark threw great parties—there is something to be said for watching the fireworks from an air conditioned apartment. Washington is hot and sticky in July! He and Kathy now have adorable two-year old twins, Alex and Katie, but still find time to entertain graciously.

Our friend Mike, (of Mr. P's Smokey Pecans, page 86) is also a great entertainer. He can whip up anything that not only tastes great but is also creatively styled on the serving dishes and the table. He is an original member of the Dirt Club and the members (Bob, Bert, Dick, Craig, Ron, Mark, Steve and Tom, Bob's brother who is the perpetual pledge) love to have the monthly meetings at his house. They always know they are in for a gourmet meal. You might be wondering, "What in the heck is the Dirt Club!?" Just turn the page and find out.

Sometimes you want a sacred night with the guys to hang out, eat, drink, smoke cigars and do guys' stuff. My friends Bob and Mike formed the Dirt Club many years ago. The eight original members have known each other since college, high school or in some instances grammar school. Each one is a successful professional. Bob and Mike have me in stitches with their stories.

Here are the rules: there are no rules; the members are shallow and can be bought. You can be on double secret probation and you don't even know it until you've been "pink shirted." Yes, there is one pink shirt and one can be awarded the pink shirt for a variety of reasons such as neglecting fellow members (getting "pink shirted" is not a good thing). The "pink shirtee" must wear the shirt to every meeting and cannot wash it between meetings.

The Dirt Club Annual Meeting is a spring golf outing to Myrtle Beach that Bob springs for (needless to say, Bob has never been "pink shirted." When threatened his response is, "I have two words: 'Myrtle Beach.'"). At the Annual Meeting the new president is elected. One year the outgoing president didn't adequately fulfill the obligations of the office, so he was punished and elected president for a second term.

Members rotate hosting monthly meetings. The host usually orders in dinner and provides an open bar and cigars. Not Mike, he goes all out. They love the meetings at Mike's.

Oh, the Super Bowl. Whether or not you like the teams playing it's a must watch. It's a guy's duty.

Chili and chicken wings on a Super Bowl Party menu are as traditional as turkey for Thanksgiving or corned beef for St. Patrick's day. Here is a traditional Super Bowl Party menu.

I'm not sure when the Super Bowl turned into an all day affair with coverage starting at 10:00 am for a 6:30 pm kick off. Some years the game itself is actually good, other years the commercials far outweigh the game. This year was a record setter—the Janet Jackson/Justin Timberlake shock and awe took the cake. I watched the whole game and I can't tell you which teams played in it, nor do I remember any of the commercials. But I can tell you what happened during the half time show. We were at a party at Pat and Bridget's and it must have been TiVoed a hundred times. Maybe the Super Bowl has turned into such a commercial venture it's the new platform for having a tasteless 15 minute halftime show so celebrities can get more PR. What happened to the days of the marching band?

I remember one year the game was particularly good, as were the commercials. No one wanted to pull themselves away from the TV for a restroom break for fear of missing a great commercial. I think Charmin should sponsor a 60 second commercial just showing a package of Charmin and the text, "This break brought to you by Charmin."

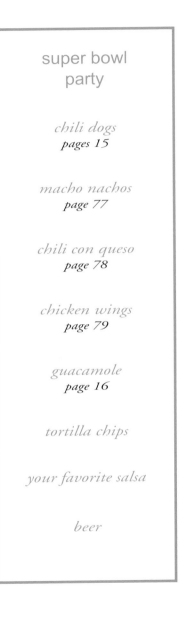

super bowl
party

chili dogs
pages 15

macho nachos
page 77

chili con queso
page 78

chicken wings
page 79

guacamole
page 16

tortilla chips

your favorite salsa

beer

picnic

roasted cashews

spiced shrimp
page 87

roasted chicken and
pesto sandwiches
page 26

brooklyn potato salad
page 19

marinated mushrooms
page 84

drunken melon
page 89

chilled white wine

You've been dating that someone special for a couple of months. It's a Thursday night and has been a hectic week at work for both of you. Why not get an early start on the weekend and surprise her with a romantic evening under the stars at a "Concert in the Park?" If it's a nice evening out, who even cares about what the concert is—it's just relaxing to sit under the stars on a beautiful evening, lie back and enjoy the moonlit sky.

This menu can be prepared the night before. I'd suggest waiting until the day of to assemble the chicken sandwiches. If you make them the night before they will probably get soggy. Get a fresh baguette the day of and make the sandwiches just before heading out.

If this is a spur of the moment event, and you don't have left over roasted chicken in the refrigerator, and if you don't have time to roast one, don't worry. On your way home from work stop at the market and pick up a roasted chicken (most grocery stores have them already roasted in the deli section). You may want to buy prepared potato salad or substitute fancy chips instead such as Terra Chips (which look like wonderfully colored potato chips made from vegetables like beets and sweet potatoes).

Pack your picnic, grab a blanket and your lady and enjoy the evening.

The football fanatic is a species unto itself. It is amazing how an otherwise seemingly "normal" person can morph into a football fanatic on Saturdays and Sundays from September through January. The fanatic's world revolves around his team—faces painted with the team colors, decked out in logoed hats, jerseys, coats, sweatshirts, tee shirts, socks, oversized #1 sponge fingers, sporting team banners on their cars and carrying logoed seat cushions, blankets, cups and homemade signs. Thank God for the football fan!

I am so glad Joe Gibbs is coming back to the Redskins! And so are millions of other Redskins fans. I just love going to home games on a chilly fall afternoon and making a day of it and I am going to love it even more now that Gibbs is back in town.

I enjoy preparing a tailgate, and for Denise and me to meet friends in the parking lot, toss around the pigskin while tossing back a few cold ones, snacking on shelled peanuts and chicken wings while grilling up some brats.

I have seen tailgate parties with white linen table cloths, grilled tenderloin and lobster tails—really first class fare. There's nothing wrong with that, but I happen to like the basics. Somehow it just doesn't seem right to me to be dining like that when I'm wearing my #9 Sonny Jurgenson jersey and blue jeans.

Go 'Skins!

tailgate

peanuts, shells on

chicken wings
page 79

bratwurst
page 112

sauerkraut

mustard

chopped onions

cold beer

peppermint schnapps

This is the big night. You're going to meet her parents for the first time and you really want to impress them. Preparing a full dinner might be a bit cumbersome for this particular evening—you want to spend time getting to know them, not be in the kitchen. This is a really nice way for you to entertain them at your place before treating them to a special dinner at your favorite restaurant.

Champagne and a few hors d'oeuvres at your place will set the tone for the evening and leave them with a very favorable first impression. Create a special mood for the evening. Chill a good bottle of champagne, such as Veuve Cliquot or Moet. If you don't have champagne flutes, this might be the perfect time to make the investment. Buy some special cocktail napkins and fresh flowers. Create a welcoming atmosphere by dimming the lights, lighting a few candles and having soft music playing in the background.

Arrange the shrimp skewers on an attractive plate and put the smoky pecans in a small dish. Arrange the shrimp plate, pecans, cocktail napkins, flowers and champagne flutes on the coffee table. When the parents arrive and after introductions pop the champagne. I guarantee they will have a very favorable first impression of you and know their daughter is in good hands.

Good luck and congratulations!

Denise and I met in January 2003. By the time we spent our first Christmas together we were engaged and I wanted the holiday season to be really memorable. We cut down a live Christmas tree and I decorated my house for the holiday. I played "The Twelve Days of Christmas" for Denise and gave her a present a day starting on December 14th. I wanted to make Christmas Eve really special so I planned a special dinner. I set a beautiful table in front of a roaring fire, had wonderful appetizers, chilled champagne, Christmas music playing, and was making my favorite dinner before heading off to midnight Mass. Denise arrived looking beautiful as always. I was very proud of myself—I paid attention to every detail to make this a memorable Christmas Eve. The evening was perfect except for one tiny thing. Denise had a raging fever and the flu and didn't want me to know. She pretended she was fine but when she wasn't drinking her champagne I knew something was wrong (she *never* passes on good champagne). She just lay on the couch, no appetite, no desire for champagne. I know she felt badly for me that I had gone to so much trouble. She was a good sport and picked at my carefully prepared dinner.

Little did I know this evening was a prelude of times to come. To this day, she still gets sick at the most inopportune times.

This was my menu for our first Christmas Eve.

dinner for two

assorted cheeses and crackers

roasted cashews

breaded pork chops
page 101

mashed potatoes
page 20

steamed broccoli
page 31

sauerkraut

apple sauce

chocolate truffles

champagne

popcorn

movie theater candy
Sno-caps
Whoppers
Raisinets
Goobers
Jujyfruits
Twizzlers
Milk Duds
Junior Mints

assorted sodas

pizza
page 82

pizza toppings
pepperoni
mushrooms
sausage
peppers
onions
spinach
pineapple
olives
artichokes
shrimp

You've got the kids for the weekend *and* their friends. What are you going to do for fun? Movie night is a great idea. This isn't just any movie night of plopping in front of the TV all night. This movie night involves a double feature, movie theater candy and everyone making their own pizza. Why is it that some candies we only eat at the movie theater? I wouldn't think of buying Milk Duds in the grocery store. I wouldn't *not* think of buying them at the movie theater. Think about it, when was the last time you bought Sno-Caps or Goobers *not* at the movie theater? Target has a movie theater candy section where you can stock up for this occasion.

Have an assortment of movies to watch. The majority rules when it comes to selecting what to watch. Start the evening early, say at 4:00. Serve popcorn, sodas and movie theater candy (watch the little teeth and fillings on the Jujyfruits). After the first movie, during "intermission" engage everyone by letting them fix their own pizza. Use 6-inch pita bread for crusts so each pizza is an individual serving. Make it fun by having a contest for the most creative pizza.

Eat the pizza while showing the second half of the double feature.

Enjoy your evening with the kids.

An after hours breakfast is really fun to do. I have fond memories of summer breaks during college. A group of us would get together and throw fun parties. We'd rent out the Elks Club, hire a DJ, get several kegs, charge $5 and have a couple of hundred people dancing the night away to Carolina beach music and classic Motown. Afterward a bunch of us would end up at my parents' house for an after hours breakfast. Bob Moran, who was not yet married to my sister Missy, was always in attendance and loved to help in the kitchen. The "appetizer" was mini donuts. Morton used to make frozen mini one-bite cinnamon sugar donuts to be heated on a pan for 10 minutes. They were so crispy on the outside and soft on the inside. I could eat a dozen! On one occasion Bob was in charge of the donuts and forgot about them once he put them in the oven, until it was too late. They burned and left indelible little circles on the pan. We laughed! My mom still has the pan and the donut circles are still on it. Every time we're at her house and she uses "The Bob Moran Memorial Donut Pan" we have a good laugh about those days. I wish Morton still made those donuts and I wish I could stay up late enough to have one of these breakfasts again.

Bake the coffee cake the day before and have it ready when the guests arrive. Prepare the casseroles earlier in the day. Bake them once guests arrive and make the home fries while the casseroles bake.

after hours breakfast

pull apart coffee cake
page 51

breakfast casserole
page 46

grits casserole
page 50

home fries
page 47

cut-up fruit

mimosas
page 133

bloody marys
page 130

coffee

I was on a guy's ski weekend with the usual suspects—Carter, Joe and Don. We stayed at my time-share complete with its own tiny kitchen. Among the assortment of munchies on hand was a five pound bag of pistachios, several pounds of spiced shrimp, and a roasting chicken.

Joe, hungover, stayed back and roasted the chicken while we hit the slopes for a morning of skiing. At midday we came back to check on Joe and his chicken and grab a beverage. Joe's roasted chicken was so tempting to starving skiers we immediately started picking at it. In fact we were picking at whatever we could put our hands on—the pistachios sitting in the bowl on the counter and the spiced shrimp Carter pulled out of the fridge. We deglazed the roasting pan with red wine, poured the sauce in a bowl, plopped the chicken on a platter and placed the chicken and sauce in the middle of the table and announced we were having a "chicken pick" for lunch.

We ended up with an impromptu pickin' party. We just picked at everything—the pistachios, shrimp and chicken.

5 pounds of nuts: $12
3 pounds of shrimp: $18
1 big fat roasting chicken: $10
Pickin' party with the buds: priceless!

P.S. I sneaked a bowl of my famous Billy's chili.

As the saying goes, "What happens in Las Vegas stays in Las Vegas." So goes the bachelor party—what happens at the bachelor party stays at the bachelor party.

Your buddy is getting married and you're the best man. The pressure is on to throw a bachelor party. They run the gamut and typically start out civilized; how they end up is another story and not to be published.

Barney, my best man, planned an all day affair and different people joined in different parts of the party. We started out with lunch at the club and tee times for several foursomes. Plenty of beer, cigars and betting was involved.

After golf, a limo picked us up and we went to dinner then several other establishments. We ended the night back at my house; Linda, Barney's wife, had prepared the after hours munchees for us, and boy, did we need them!

I had my first cigar that night and was I ever sick! I learned a cigar is an acquired taste, like bourbon. As I finally did with bourbon, I had no problem eventually acquiring a taste for fine cigars.

bachelor party

tee time

assorted nuts

bill's famous bacon and horseradish dip
page 85

potato chips

club sandwiches
page 57

dad's bronx appetizer
page 81

grills with
page 88

cigars

a limo

cash

coffee